Scripture and the Wesleyan Way

Scripture and the Wesleyan Way
A Bible Study on Real Christianity

Book
978-1-5018-6793-4
978-1-5018-6794-1 eBook

DVD
978-1-5018-6797-2

Leader Guide
978-1-5018-6795-8
978-1-5018-6796-5 eBook

For more information, visit AbingdonPress.com.

Also by Scott J. Jones and Arthur D. Jones

Ask: Faith Questions in a Skeptical Age

Also by Scott J. Jones

The Wesleyan Way: A Faith That Matters

The Once and Future Wesleyan Movement

*The Future of The United Methodist Church:
Seven Vision Pathways* (Ed. with Bruce Ough)

Staying at the Table: The Gift of Unity for United Methodists

*The Evangelistic Love of God and Neighbor:
A Theology of Witness and Discipleship*

United Methodist Doctrine: The Extreme Center

John Wesley's Conception and Use of Scripture

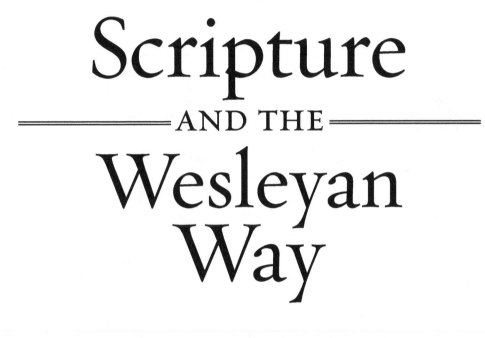

Scripture
AND THE
Wesleyan Way

A Bible Study on Real Christianity

SCOTT J. JONES AND ARTHUR D. JONES

Abingdon Press / Nashville

Scripture and the Wesleyan Way
A Bible Study on Real Christianity

Copyright © 2018 Abingdon Press

Library of Congress Cataloging-in-Publication data has been requested.

978-1-5018-6793-4

Scripture quotations unless noted otherwise are taken from the Common English Bible, copyright 2011. Used by permission. All rights reserved.

Scripture quotations noted NRSV are from New Revised Standard Version Bible, copyright © 1989 National Council of the Churches of Christ in the United States of America. Used by permission. All rights reserved worldwide. http://nrsvbibles.org/

Scripture quotations marked (ESV) are from the ESV Bible (The Holy Bible, English Standard Version®), copyright © 2001 by Crossway, a publishing ministry of Good News Publishers. Used by permission. All rights reserved.

Scripture quotations noted KJV are taken from The Authorized (King James) Version. Rights in the Authorized Version in the United Kingdom are vested in the Crown. Reproduced by permission of the Crown's patentee, Cambridge University Press.

Quotations noted *Sermons* are from *John Wesley's Sermons: An Anthology*, eds. Albert C. Outler and Richard P. Heitzenrater. Nashville: Abingdon, 1991.

Quotations noted *The UM Hymnal* are from *The United Methodist Hymnal: Book of United Methodist Worship*. Nashville: The United Methodist Publishing House, 1989.

Quotations noted *Book of Discipline* are from *The Book of Discipline of The United Methodist Church, 2016*. Nashville: The United Methodist Publishing House, 2016.

Quotations noted *JW Works* are from *The Works of John Wesley*, Bicentennial Edition, Nashville: Abingdon Press.

18 19 20 21 22 23 24 25 26 27 — 10 9 8 7 6 5 4 3 2 1
MANUFACTURED IN THE UNITED STATES OF AMERICA

Table of Contents

Introduction

John Wesley created something new by trying something very old: to take the early church and its Scriptures seriously. He said that he wanted nothing more than "primitive Christianity," which simply means a restoration of the church as it is now to the power and depth of the early church. Wesleyans focus a lot upon Wesley not because we believe Wesley was always right, but because he is the right guide to help us read Scripture faithfully and to renew the church.

Everyone needs guides. God's actions and messages through the Bible are so expansive that to understand the whole story of Scripture and where Jesus fits in, we need guides to help us navigate it. From the moment Jesus ascended into heaven, we Christians have modeled our own examples and our thoughts after those whose examples and thoughts most closely followed Jesus—they are our guides. Peter began with this as he led the church in Jerusalem. Soon, others were following Jesus so closely that they became the first saints of the church. Paul wrote in his letter to the Corinthians encouraging them to follow him—*not* so that they would become like him, but that they would become like Jesus through his example: "I don't look out for my own advantage, but I look out for many people so that they can be saved. Follow my example, just like I follow Christ's" (1 Corinthians 10:33b–11:1).

When we follow the example of John Wesley and his brother Charles, we do (for the most part) follow the example of Jesus. While it is clear that they made mistakes and in some areas got it wrong, they had a great deal of insight into how to be Christian in the modern world. We believe that when we read the Scriptures with the mindset of these Wesley brothers, we are confronted with the entirety of Scripture as the story of God's efforts to redeem all of us in a manner that resembles Jesus' message. It demands of us a response to *actually* love God and to *actually* love our neighbor—even our enemies— as we love ourselves, as did Jesus. This means to us that the Wesleyan way of reading Scripture is both practical and faithful. In the same way that Jesus' message was not a theological treatise, but rather a practical conversation with people in need of grace, the Wesleyan approach to the Bible focuses on what Scripture was meant to be: a gift of "divine inspiration" to you and me.

As we study the Bible with Wesley, it is important to remember that the primary goal is not to read Wesley well, but to read Scripture well. It is the Bible that is authoritative, not the teaching of the Wesley brothers. However, there are many ways of reading Scripture and we have found a Wesleyan perspective to be the most helpful guide through the Bible. In his book *Orthodoxy*, G. K. Chesterton describes the power of Christian theology when it matches God with the needs of the world: "[A] strange thing began to happen. When once these two parts of the two machines had come together, one after another, all the other parts fitted and fell in with an eerie exactitude." This is how we feel about Wesleyan doctrine. It makes a complicated Bible and faith make sense in our daily lives.

Due to the practical nature of Jesus and John Wesley, this Bible study will begin with spiritual questions, look at the biblical texts that deal with these questions, and then show how Wesley applied those Scriptures to answer the questions and illuminate the larger story of God's salvation. Consider the last chapter in this book, the use of money. It is based on one of the more perplexing Scriptures, that, taken at face value, seems rather odd: "I tell you, use worldly wealth to make friends for yourselves so that when it's gone, you will be welcomed into the eternal homes" (Luke 16:9). When you read the Bible alongside Wesley, you are not left to your own devices to understand this passage. You are led to consider the other ways that Jesus spoke about money, as well as the Christian truths behind generosity. Through imitating Wesley's approach to Scripture, you are led to develop a way to understand the larger view of God's purposes for money in Scripture. With this approach, we believe that you can learn to understand the Bible, and therefore Jesus, better.

Wesley's goal wasn't to have a comprehensive analysis of Scripture, but rather to use Scripture the way Jesus did. Jesus sought to help those he met become more faithful by fulfilling the greatest and the second greatest commandments—to love God and love neighbor—and Wesley sought the same thing. If you find you read Scripture and aren't becoming more like Jesus, Wesley would say you are reading it wrong.

Throughout this book we are using the label "Wesleyan" because we think we are sharing a perspective that is authentically part of the Wesleyan stream of Christianity. Not all Methodists will agree with us, but we are convinced that our connection to the thoughts of John and Charles Wesley are true to their intent.

We hope you love God and love your neighbor more through this study.

Scott and Arthur Jones

1

What Is the Bible's Message?

The Spiritual Question and Its Importance Today

The Bible is both important and complicated. So what is its message?

Christians believe the Bible is the inspired word of God that communicates truths that are essential for human beings to live well. Through it we learn who God is, who human beings are, and how to live our lives in ways that are pleasing to the Ultimate Reality of the universe. The Bible gives us insights that are available to us in no other way, and encountering God through its words is the best way to learn how to be truly happy.

Christians believe God chose Abraham and Sarah centuries ago to be the parents of a special people. Their descendants would be blessed, and through them all the nations of the earth would be blessed (Genesis 12:2-3). Through many difficulties, including time in slavery in Egypt and a difficult Exodus, they arrived at a promised land and flourished. But more trouble came to them, and exile to Babylon was part of their history. In the fullness of time a descendent of King David was born, and the turning point of all human history occurred with the birth of God's Son, Jesus.

The Bible is the authoritative account of God's interaction with the people of Israel and the first generations of Jesus' disciples. It is our written record of God's self-revelation to human beings. As United Methodist doctrine puts it, "We believe the Holy Bible, Old and New Testaments, reveals the Word of God so far as it is necessary for our salvation. It is to be received through the Holy Spirit as the true rule and guide for faith and practice."[1]

At the same time, the Bible is complicated. Our Protestant Bible has sixty-six books written over a thousand-year period in three different languages. Very few of us read it in the original languages, and even then, we sometimes don't understand the cultural references and situations that the authors were addressing. It contains many types of literature, including historical narratives, prophetic speeches, poetry, letters, and apocalyptic writings. The Bible has a diversity of literary forms, comes to us from ancient times, and contains the work of many different human authors. It is complicated.

We want to know the Bible's message because it is important, yet we struggle to understand the message because it is complicated.

Because it is both diverse and ancient, there are some interesting emphases within the Bible. Very important questions sometimes appear to have contradictory answers depending on which verses one chooses to quote. Christians in the twenty-first century would like to be able to say, "The Bible says . . ." and use its authority to settle important questions we face. Yet, someone else can sometimes respond by quoting another part of the Scriptures with a different answer. Beginning in the 1500s, Protestants argued that the Bible was clear and its message could be understood by laypersons who should read it in their own languages. Over time, this led to many different interpretations and the splintering of the Christian church into a large number of denominations. The complexity of the Bible allows many different Christian churches to claim scriptural authority for their divergent positions.

All of us believe the Bible is important. We also know it is complicated. Which leads to the question, "What is the Bible's message?" We want to know the Bible's message because it is important, yet we struggle to understand the message because it is complicated. John Wesley can guide us in answering that question. Before turning to him, let's first think about four principles which underlie Wesley's answer to the question.

First, we believe that the whole Bible is Scripture.

Sometimes in the history of Christianity persons have suggested kicking certain books out of the Bible. And it is true that Catholics and Protestants disagree about seven books in the Old Testament that Catholics count and Protestants (following Jewish practice) do not. Such major and formal revisions to the Bible are rare. Typically, attempts to revise the Bible so far have not succeeded with churches that continue to be identified as Christian. Revising the canon, either by addition (such as the Mormons did) or deletion means that your church has chosen to leave Christianity behind and form a new religion.

Almost all of the Christians in the world claim the whole Bible to be the inspired word of God and authoritative for determining Christian faith and practice. But that means they have to decide how the whole Bible fits together.

Almost all of the Christians in the world claim the whole Bible to be the inspired word of God and authoritative for determining Christian faith and practice. But that means they have to decide how the whole Bible fits together.

Scholars over the last two hundred years have emphasized careful, critical understanding of how the various books came to be written and how the canon was formed. (The canon is the list of books that are understood as Scripture.) By focusing on individual books, they can gain great insight into the meaning of each verse and clarify both how and why it was written. Such scholarly progress has tended to key in on the different emphases and concerns that each biblical author expressed in his writing.

Partly growing out of such helpful scholarship, some persons have suggested that difficult passages, especially those in the Old Testament, be sorted into different buckets. One bucket might represent God's will for all time. Another might represent God's will for a particular time, and a third bucket never represented God's will but reflected the cultures in the times where they were written. By identifying and distinguishing between these buckets, such an approach is intended to help present-day Christians cope with difficult passages in the Old Testament.

The problem with a multi-bucket approach like this is that it fails to consider how the whole Bible fits together and how the same God has worked out the same purposes in many different cultures and periods of history. The Bible fits into just two sections—an old covenant and a new covenant—and the apostles settled how to interpret the relationship between them at the Jerusalem Council recorded in Acts 15.

Sometimes people say that the Holy Spirit is still speaking today and teaching us to reject parts of the Bible that they believe should never have been included in the first place. A Wesleyan approach presumes that God has not changed God's mind and that the Holy Spirit who speaks today is the same Holy Spirit that inspired the biblical authors.

The church's job is to understand God's intent in inspiring these writings and how they all fit together rather than separate them into different buckets. The biblical authors were inspired by the Holy Spirit at a level much more directly connected to God than anything since apostolic times. Yet, we believe that the Holy Spirit is still at work, confirming in people's minds what the inspired text says and helping people interpret it correctly. We believe that the Old Testament is not contrary to the New, because salvation through Christ is offered in both parts of the Bible. The next three principles help Christians see the wholeness of the Bible.

Second, we interpret the Old Testament in light of the New Testament.

Although they were slow to fully understand who he was and what God was doing, the apostles eventually came to believe that Jesus was the Messiah, the Son of the living God (Matthew 16:16), the Word of God in human flesh (John 1:1). In him, God had done something new and different. In him, God was "reconciling the world to himself" (2 Corinthians 5:19). The

Book of Hebrews makes this very clear in its account of the saints of the Old Testament in Hebrews 11 and 12. After recounting many stories from the Old Testament, the author of Hebrews says they acted in faith and they are now part of the great cloud of witnesses surrounding us.

Yet, the earliest disciples remained Jews committed to following the law. They believed that Christ's coming was the fulfillment of the law and the promises made by the prophets.

Then a crisis happened. Jesus had made it a practice to reach out to Gentiles, and he had commanded his followers to make disciples of all nations. They were to be his witnesses to the ends of the earth. But what happens when Gentiles receive the Holy Spirit and become Jesus followers? Do they have to obey the commandments of the Old Testament?

Acts 15 records the Jerusalem Council where an important decision was made. The question was whether Gentiles who had received the Holy Spirit and accepted Christ as Lord and Savior needed to become Jews to become part of the church. Becoming Jewish meant following all of the laws in the Old Testament as they had been codified by the rabbis. This meant circumcision for men and obeying the Jewish dietary laws, among other things. The apostles and church leaders gathered in Jerusalem and communicated their final decision in a letter to the new Gentile believers: "The Holy Spirit has led us to the decision that no burden should be placed on you other than these essentials: refuse food offered to idols, blood, the meat from strangled animals, and sexual immorality. You will do well to avoid such things" (Acts 15:28-29). From this time on, the church taught that certain laws in the Old Testament were not binding on Christians. Later leaders discerned that there were three kinds of laws in the Old Testament. Christ had set aside two of them: the ceremonial laws and the civil laws. Only the moral laws are binding for Christians.

Third, we believe that the Holy Spirit has led the church to understand the Bible.

The Jerusalem Council was only the first of many times that a difficult question faced Jesus' followers. They had to consult with Jesus' teachings and seek the guidance of the Holy Spirit to decide how best to be faithful to the gospel of Christ. After the apostles had died, it was the Holy Scriptures that were consulted and interpreted as the basis of the decisions. Some of the most difficult questions were finally decided in the fourth century when bishops from all over the church came together in the Councils of Nicaea and Constantinople. There they used the Bible to formulate creeds that would summarize the Bible's teaching and settle disputed questions. One such question was how to think of God. The Old Testament taught clearly that there is only one God, but in the New Testament Jesus is called "Lord" and the Holy Spirit is worshiped. Many individuals voiced their opinions on these matters, but it was the whole church as represented by their leaders that decided how the Bible was to be interpreted, leading to the doctrine of the Trinity in which we believe in one God in three persons.

Even today Christians who belong to a church rely on their church's teaching authority to interpret Scripture for the whole community.

Even today Christians who belong to a church rely on their church's teaching authority to interpret Scripture for the whole community. Wesleyans look to the early church as especially authoritative. At the same time, modern denominations have their doctrines that pastors are supposed to teach. For The United Methodist Church, it is our Articles of Religion, the Confession of Faith, John Wesley's Sermons (as highlighted in this study), his Notes on the New Testament, and the General Rules that form the standards of United Methodist interpretation of the Bible.

Fourth, reason and experience help us understand the Bible.

John Wesley believed that Scripture was authoritative for Christian teaching and that it should be interpreted by the best parts of tradition. But he also acknowledged that reason and experience help us understand God's word. In particular, modern science has helped us see that God's revelation to people three thousand years ago was accommodated to what they could understand. Our knowledge of the universe is better than theirs, and we should look for the spiritual meaning of the text rather than a literal meaning that contradicts scientific truth. For instance, Wesleyans have no trouble accepting the spiritual truth of Genesis 1 and 2 while still affirming the conclusions of modern science about how the world has come into being over time. In the same way, we know that our experiences of God and culture sometimes shape how we read the Bible and provide deep insight into what the Holy Spirit is teaching. We can also see how God's revelation was given to human beings with very different cultural experiences and how that has shaped the biblical text.

In short, the quadrilateral of an authoritative Scripture interpreted by tradition, reason, and experience helps Wesleyans read the Scripture in accordance with God's purposes for us.

Throughout the Gospels of Matthew, Mark, and Luke, his teaching about the Kingdom is central to Jesus' message and ministry.

The Bible's Teaching

Perhaps the most important message of the New Testament, and thus of the whole Bible, concerns the kingdom of God. Jesus began his ministry preaching that the kingdom of God is at hand. In Mark 1:15, he says, "Now is the time! Here comes God's kingdom! Change your hearts and lives, and trust this good news!" Throughout the Gospels of Matthew, Mark, and Luke, his teaching about the Kingdom is central to Jesus' message and ministry. Matthew 4:23 summarizes his ministry by saying "Jesus traveled throughout Galilee, teaching in their synagogues. He announced the good news of the kingdom and healed every disease and sickness among the people." In Matthew 10:7, he sent out his disciples saying, "As you go, make this announcement: 'The kingdom of heaven has come near.'" Jesus told many parables about the Kingdom to teach his followers what it was like. In them he compares the Kingdom to:

- A farmer who scatters seed—Matthew 13:3-23
- Wheat and weeds—Matthew 13:24-30
- A mustard seed—Matthew 13:31-32
- Yeast—Matthew 13:33
- A treasure in a field—Matthew 13:44
- A pearl of great value—Matthew 13:45-46
- Fishing for many kinds of fish—Matthew 13:47-50

When Peter is given authority after he confesses that Jesus is the Messiah, Jesus says, "I'll give you the keys of the kingdom of heaven. Anything you fasten on earth will be fastened in heaven. Anything you loosen on earth will be loosened in heaven" (Matthew 16:19). Though these examples come from Matthew, parallel passages in Mark and Luke confirm that the kingdom of heaven or the kingdom of God was at the heart of Jesus' teaching and ministry.

Another indicator of how important the kingdom of God is for our faith comes in the Lord's Prayer. Regularly Christians pray, "Thy kingdom come, thy will be done on earth as it is in heaven." Such a prayer longs for conditions in this world to conform to the will of God. Jesus often painted a word picture of what our world would be like if the Kingdom did truly come. In one such picture, the parable of the sheep and the goats, the king comes to sit in judgment. Those who fed the hungry, clothed the naked, gave water to the thirsty, welcomed the stranger, and visited those who were sick and in prison were told they would inherit the Kingdom. Those who failed to care for "the least of these" were sent to eternal punishment (Matthew 25:31-46).

This vision of the kingdom of God has its roots in the Old Testament in two ways. First, it reflects obedience to the commandments that Israel should take care of the needy among them. Leviticus 23:22 says, "When you harvest your land's produce, you must not harvest all the way to the edge of your field; and don't gather every remaining bit of your harvest. Leave these items for the poor and the immigrant; I am the LORD your God." Many commandments reminded Israel that they had once been slaves and needed to care for the underprivileged. The laws of Israel in the first five books of the Bible often addressed how the poor were to be cared for by the community and how justice was to be a hallmark of Israel's character.

Second, the concern for the poor was later conveyed by the prophets who continually delivered to Israel God's demands for justice. They were often outraged at the way in which the least of these were treated by the wealthy and powerful in Israel and they pronounced God's judgment on God's chosen people for failing to implement the laws. When Jesus spoke about the kingdom of God, he was reinforcing the same message that the prophets had delivered centuries earlier.

This vision of the Kingdom was related to how the role of king was perceived in the Old Testament. It was the job of the kings of Israel to guarantee that God's chosen people would follow God's will. In part, this meant maintaining purity of worship and keeping out false religious practices. But it was also the job of the king to ensure obedience to the law. Kingship was established by Samuel, who can be characterized as either the last judge or the first prophet. Leaders of Israel wanted a king like the other nations. Speaking for God, Samuel warned them how they would be treated by a king, and yet they wanted one anyway. So God led Samuel to anoint first Saul and then David as kings over Israel. Eventually, there grew up a belief that David's descendants would rule over Israel forever. As Israel and Judah lost their independence and became subservient to other empires, the hope for an anointed king or messiah was born. Such a king would be a descendant of David. Thus, Jesus was greeted on his entry into Jerusalem as the son of David who would save his people and establish the Kingdom.

For those seeking to follow Jesus centuries later, understanding the kingdom of God is an important aspect of our faith.

Much of the drama of Jesus' last week before his death and resurrection was caused by the misunderstanding about the nature of his kingship and the content of the good news he was preaching. Even at his ascension the disciples asked him, "Lord, are you going to restore the kingdom to Israel now?" (Acts 1:6). For those seeking to follow Jesus centuries later, understanding the kingdom of God is an important aspect of our faith.

Wesley's Answer

What is the Bible's message? John Wesley in his sermon "The Way to the Kingdom" teaches that the Bible's message concerns the kingdom of God. Each of Wesley's sermons has a biblical text and this one uses only one verse, Mark 1:15, which Wesley quotes from the King James Version: "The kingdom of God is at hand: repent ye, and believe the gospel." In addition to this main text, though, Wesley almost always quotes or alludes to many different biblical texts in each sermon. Here he quickly introduces a second one, Romans 14:17: "The kingdom of God is not meat and drink; but righteousness, and peace, and joy in the Holy Ghost" (KJV).

Wesley's overriding concern in interpreting the Bible is how a person can be saved from sin and for salvation. His approach is based on the importance of the kingdom of God in Jesus' preaching as shown in the Mark passage and the clear definition of it given in the Romans passage. For Wesley, the kingdom of God is a state of the individual's soul. He explicitly is talking about religion of the heart.

Wesley begins the sermon by identifying the question as, What is the nature of true religion? For him, religion is a good thing and the purpose of all his sermons is to clarify what real religion, specifically real Christianity, is all about. The Romans passage is helpful because it specifically says what true religion is not—it is not "meat and drink."

Wesley takes these words as referring to the ceremonial law of Moses. He wanted to make sure that true religion was understood not to rely on any ceremonies or rules like what someone can eat or what offerings need to be made. All such rituals prescribed in the Old Testament had been effectively set aside by the Jerusalem Council to the point that true religion cannot be said to require any particular ceremonies at all. While this is true of the rules required by the Old Testament, it is especially true of rules written by human beings.

Wesley goes further to say that the religion of Jesus Christ also does not consist of orthodoxy or right opinions. He argues that orthodoxy, or believing correctly, is a matter of one's understanding and not the heart. He suggests that a person can fully subscribe to all the doctrines of Christianity—God, Christ, the Trinity, salvation, and the creeds—without truly having faith. He even notes that the devil believes correctly with no errors in his understanding. James 2:19 says that demons know the truth and they tremble.

So far Wesley is criticizing nominal Christians. They believe that being Christian is constituted by holding certain beliefs, affirming the creeds, and following the rules of behavior like attending worship, giving money, and avoiding evil practices. In the first two pages of his sermon, Wesley says it is possible to do all of these things and have no genuine religion at all. How can this be?

Christianity is a religion of the heart.

This logical pattern shows up in many of Wesley's sermons and arguments. He will circle around and later talk about how correct belief and these practices of the faith have their place. But he wants to get clear about the essential and most important part of true religion. For Wesley, Christianity is a religion of the heart. He relies on the Romans 14 description that the kingdom of God is "righteousness, and peace, and joy in the Holy Ghost" (KJV).

Righteousness means loving God with all your heart, soul, mind, and strength, which Jesus called the first and greatest commandment (Mark 12:30 NRSV). Someone with this kind of righteousness truly loves God with everything one has. But Jesus also coupled the love of neighbor with this kind of righteousness. Wesley is clear that such love is an attitude of the heart whereby one desires the best for the other person, including one's family and friends, but also people whom one does not know and persons whom one knows to be evil and undeserving. Persons who experience this kind of love exhibit "compassion, kindness, humility, gentleness, and patience" (Colossians 3:12).

True religion of the heart also means peace. Wesley makes reference to the "peace of God that exceeds all understanding" (Philippians 4:7). Doubt and uncertainty are gone, and the believer has no fear because of his or her confidence in Christ. The Holy Spirit bears witness with our spirit that we are children of God and heirs of God's promises. That gives us a sense of peace that casts out our fears.

Such love and peace then produce joy. Wesley quotes Psalm 32:1, "Blessed is the man whose unrighteousness is forgiven." In an important parenthetical remark, he substitutes the word "happy" for blessed. The Common English Bible translation renders that verse as, "The one whose wrongdoing is forgiven, / whose sin is covered over, is truly happy!" When translating the Sermon on the Mount for his *Explanatory Notes Upon the New Testament*, Wesley systematically starts each of the Beatitudes with the word "happy" instead of the King James translation "blessed." Thus, his translation of Matthew 5:3 reads "Happy are the poor in spirit, for theirs is the kingdom of heaven." This substitution of "happy" for "blessed," which is still true to the original language, brings out the connotation of joy. Knowing God in this way enables the believer to be joyful. Wesley then says,

> This holiness and happiness, joined in one, are sometimes styled in the inspired writings, 'the kingdom of God' (as by our Lord in the text), and sometimes, 'the kingdom of heaven.' It is termed 'the kingdom of God' because it is the immediate fruit of God's reigning in the soul. So soon as ever he takes unto himself his mighty power, and sets up his throne in our hearts, they are instantly filled with this 'righteousness, and peace, and joy in the Holy Ghost.'[2]

Whenever the gospel of Christ is preached, the kingdom is at hand because the power of God is available to bring these characteristics to the hearts of the people. All those who hear the gospel are invited to enter into the kingdom.

Whenever the gospel of Christ is preached, the Kingdom is at hand because the power of God is available to bring these characteristics to the hearts of the people. All those who hear the gospel are invited to enter into the Kingdom.

Wesley then says, "This is the way. Walk ye in it." He turns to the two key commandments in the last half of the Mark 1:15 verse: repent and believe. Repentance is the first step whereby someone recognizes his or her need for God's forgiveness of one's sins. Recognition that one is a sinner who can never adequately atone for past misdeeds is a crucial starting place. Taking honest inventory of oneself is crucial. When we look honestly, we see that our hearts are characterized by vanity, thirst of praise, ambition, covetousness, lust of the flesh, lust of the eye, anger, hatred, malice, revenge, envy, jealousy, and other sins. Someone might want to make a different list of sins that are more applicable to his or her life. Nevertheless, for all of us, when we measure ourselves against God's intention for our lives, we have all fallen short.

Repentance is the process of naming our problem and turning our lives around. Literally, the word translated as "repent" from Hebrew means to turn. If one is headed toward hell and destruction, the crucial move is to turn around and head toward heaven and new life. The Greek word that is translated as *repent* literally means to change one's mind. It is to recognize oneself as a sinner and admit one needs God's forgiveness and power to change.

The people who know the most about repentance in American culture are the leaders of Alcoholics Anonymous. They have a saying: "You cannot help a drunk." Only when a person bottoms out and admits she or he is powerless over the addiction can that person be helped. AA members start their meetings by giving their names and saying, "I'm an alcoholic." We have known people who have been sober for twenty years and still describe themselves as an alcoholic. In the same way, lifelong Christians describe themselves as sinners in need of God's saving grace.

When we experience the love of God in that way and respond by accepting it, the kingdom of God has come to us. That is Wesley's answer to our question. That is the Bible's message.

Believing the gospel means having the kind of faith that is a sure trust and confidence in God. Saving faith is not merely assent or having the right beliefs. It is an attitude of the heart whereby God's love is poured out in our hearts (Romans 5:5). When we experience the love of God in that way and respond by accepting it, the kingdom of God has come to us. That is Wesley's answer to our question. That is the Bible's message.

The Wesleyan Way of Salvation

Wesley's description of the kingdom of God and how to live in it represents the ideal of the Christian life. We aspire to love God with all that we have and to love our neighbors as ourselves. We would like to be at peace and free from fear. We read 1 Thessalonians 5:16 and we want to "rejoice always." We read 2 Corinthians 5:6, which says "we are always confident," and we aspire to live that way.

But what about the times when Christians do not experience "righteousness, peace, and joy in the Holy Spirit" (Romans 14:17)? There are dark nights of the soul where our faith is weak, God seems far away, and this description of the Christian life seems unattainable.

The Wesleyan answer is to adjust your behavior so that the kingdom of God comes near again. God is constantly seeking to give his followers these gifts; and by regular worship, Bible study, participating in small groups, and other means of grace we can experience more and more of them in our daily lives.

Wesley notes briefly in this sermon that those who experience the Kingdom in this way are immediately motivated to live in a way that serves God's purposes. True believers work to feed the hungry, clothe the naked, and bring justice to the poor. People who experience the kingdom of God will then do all in their power to change the world so that it conforms more closely to God's will for all creation, including all of humanity.

What is the Bible's message? According to Wesley, the Bible is about the kingdom of God. The essential first step in the Way to the Kingdom is for human beings to experience the life-changing love of God in Christ Jesus.

Love Divine, All Loves Excelling

The essential first step in the Way to the Kingdom is for human beings to experience the life-changing love of God in Christ Jesus. Charles Wesley's powerful hymn describes how the grace of God can change our hearts and help us find the righteousness, joy, and peace promised in the kingdom of God. When we know the love of God and respond with repentance and faith, God then changes us to become more of what God wants us to be.

Love divine, all loves excelling,
joy of heaven, to earth come down;
fix in us thy humble dwelling;
all thy faithful mercies crown!
Jesus, thou art all compassion,
pure, unbounded love thou art;
visit us with thy salvation;
enter every trembling heart.

Breathe, O breathe thy loving Spirit
into every troubled breast!
Let us all in thee inherit;
let us find that second rest.
Take away our bent to sinning;
Alpha and Omega be;
end of faith, as its beginning,
set our hearts at liberty.

Come, Almighty to deliver,
let us all thy life receive;
suddenly return and never,
nevermore thy temples leave.
Thee we would be always blessing,
serve thee as thy hosts above,
pray and praise thee without ceasing,
glory in thy perfect love.

Finish, then, thy new creation;
pure and spotless let us be.
Let us see thy great salvation
perfectly restored in thee;
changed from glory into glory,
till in heaven we take our place,
till we cast our crowns before thee,
lost in wonder, love, and praise.[3]

2

How Can I Be Saved?

The Spiritual Question and Its Importance Today

Every now and then we hear someone tell their life story beginning with "When I got saved . . ." From some of these people the story is one of major change. There was a time when they were not following Jesus and instead they were engaging in self-destructive and immoral behaviors. Something happened to connect them to God, and at a specific time and place they had a conversion experience, accepting Christ as Lord and Savior. The negative behaviors were left behind, the person embraced a new identity as a disciple of Jesus, and he or she joined a new group called the church.

Often when someone tells a conversion story like that, it sounds very simple. We have both been asked "Are you saved?" We tend to answer "Yes, praise God," but we always want to find out more about what the questioner means by salvation.

We have both been in other conversations where other questions are posed, either out loud or barely beneath the surface. Consider the following:

- Am I OK?
- Am I loved and valued?
- Am I living a good life?
- How can I live a better life?
- After I die, what happens to me?
- Does my life have any meaning or purpose?
- What should be the purpose of my life?

We think such questions are really asking about salvation. They focus on the really big issue of how one should live one's life. Whenever someone asks one of these questions, they are venturing into the topic of what it means to be saved.

We also know people who don't have the luxury of asking such questions. They are living on the margins of society, barely existing and simply trying to stay alive by finding another day's food, paying the bills, or locating adequate shelter. As we engage in discussing such questions, what about the people who aren't even asking spiritual questions at all?

When someone asks, "Are you saved?" it appears to be a simple question. Actually, answering it is one of those simple teachings that has a lot of complexity below the surface.

The Bible's way of addressing all of these big life questions is to talk about salvation.

The Bible's Teaching

The Bible's way of addressing all of these big life questions is to talk about salvation. John 3:17 says, "God didn't send his Son into the world to judge the world, but that the world might be saved through him." The Nicene Creed says that this was the whole point of Jesus' life: "For us and for our salvation he came down from heaven, was incarnate of the Holy Spirit and the Virgin Mary and became truly human."[1] Thus, all of Jesus' preaching and teaching and all of the accounts in the New Testament could be understood as showing how people can be saved.

In Jesus' ministry, salvation is mentioned with at least four different aspects: reconciliation, restoration, healing, and resurrection. The meaning of "saved" depended on the individual he was saving.

In several cases, Christ was engaged in bringing reconciliation with God. Like John the Baptist, Jesus was preaching about how the people could have their sins forgiven and avoid the wrath of God. In Luke 7:36-50, the connection between salvation and forgiveness becomes explicit. Jesus is having dinner at the home of a Pharisee, and a sinful woman anoints Jesus' feet with ointment, washes them with her tears, and dries them with her hair. The Pharisee is bothered by the fact that Jesus allows such a woman to serve him. Jesus uses it as a teaching moment to show that those who have sinned much and are forgiven much often have greater love. He tells the woman that her sins are forgiven because of her love, and then the story closes with the Lord saying to her, "Your faith has saved you. Go in peace" (Luke 7:50).

Implied in this story is another aspect of Jesus' ministry of salvation: restoration. Sometimes salvation means not only restoring someone's relationship to God but also that person's relationship to the community of faith. Jesus' encounter with Zacchaeus illustrates how salvation means restoration back to heal broken relationships. Zacchaeus was the chief tax collector for Jericho and was very rich. Jesus went to his house for dinner, which scandalized the community. But Zacchaeus responded to Jesus by giving half of his wealth to the poor and repaying several times over those whom he had cheated. Jesus pronounced, "Today, salvation has come to this household because he too is a son of Abraham" (Luke 19:9).

Another aspect of Jesus' ministry of salvation was healing. The Gospels record Jesus healing a number of people, and in several cases their healing is referred to as their being saved. The blind man by the road in Jericho was given his sight and told "your faith has saved you" (Luke 18:42 NRSV). When Jairus asked Jesus to come and heal his daughter, she died before Jesus arrived at the house. They then told Jesus what had happened and that he no longer needed to come. Instead Jesus said, "Do not fear. Only believe, and she will be saved" (Luke 8:50 NRSV). When Jesus took her by the hand, she rose from her bed and ate. There is such a close connection between salvation and healing that the Common English Bible translation in both of these accounts substitutes "healed" for "saved."

Salvation also refers to life after death in Jesus' ministry. In John's Gospel, that is part of the meaning of resurrection and eternal life. John 3:16 says, "For God so loved the world that he gave his only Son, so that everyone who believes in him may not perish but may have eternal life" (NRSV). While hanging on the cross, Jesus was mocked by the soldiers and one of the criminals being crucified with him, who suggested that he should save himself. When the other criminal professed faith in Christ, Jesus said to him, "I assure you that today you will be with me in paradise" (Luke 23:43). Salvation here included life with Christ after death.

Jesus was concerned about the whole person.

We believe that Jesus' teaching about salvation has at least these four aspects because Jesus was concerned about the whole person. Salvation should fix whatever was wrong in their lives. For some, salvation means reconciliation with God because of their sins. For others it is restoration with the community. For others, it is physical healing, and yet for others it is life after death. For many it is all four combined.

This is the background for the preaching of the apostles in the years after Jesus' resurrection and ascension. Peter and John boldly proclaimed to the Jewish leaders that there is salvation in no one else (Acts 4:12). Paul begins his letter to the Romans by saying that he had been set apart for the gospel, which is "God's own power for salvation to all who have faith in God, to the Jew first and also to the Greek" (Romans 1:16).

Yet as the apostles sought to explain Jesus' message of salvation, a crucial tension emerged regarding salvation by faith and salvation by good works. In the Book of Romans, Paul makes a strong case that we are saved by faith. He says in Romans 3:28, "For we hold that a person is justified by faith apart from works prescribed by the law" (NRSV). Paul's argument is aimed at understanding the faithfulness of God to account for the inclusion of the Gentiles in the church. Thus, he argues that Abraham was justified by faith (Romans 4). Abraham's actions were exemplary, but he was justified not by them, but by faith. In Paul's magnificent conclusion he writes, "Therefore, since we are justified by faith . . ." (Romans 5:1 NRSV). Reading Paul alone, one might believe that good works are irrelevant to one's salvation.

But another book makes a different argument. In the Letter of James, the author exhorts the readers to "be doers of the word and not only hearers" (James 1:22). He is concerned for the poor and specifically for behaving in ways that are congruent with the salvation one has experienced. One's actions count. If someone is hungry and you fail to feed the person, you have broken that law. James argues that Abraham was justified by his works, specifically his willingness to sacrifice Isaac on the altar. He argues that faith and works go together, but that works are necessary. In James 2:17 he says, "So faith by itself, if it has no works, is dead" (NRSV).

Someone who had a bias one way or another, or someone who decided to quote only Paul or only James, might pick a one-sided way of resolving this tension. Following Paul's argument in Romans, someone might conclude, "We are saved by faith alone, and our behavior does not matter to our salvation." But someone else might focus only on James and say that it is good works that show what faith truly is, so they are what really matter to one's salvation. How can I be saved? Is it through my faith—what I believe— or through my behavior—how I live and act? Historians of Christianity can point to times and places where one side or the other of this tension has appeared to predominate.

Wesley's Answer

Wesley's approach is best described as occupying the extreme center, holding together both sides of the tension at the same time. His sermon "The Scripture Way of Salvation" is one of his clearest statements of how he balances what in some interpretations is a biblical contradiction.

Wesley finds ways of affirming two or more ideas that other people see as mutually exclusive.

Wesley's interpretation of faith versus works, his view of the church, and his understanding of the Christian life frequently have this extreme center approach. He finds ways of affirming two or more ideas that other people see as mutually exclusive. It would be accurate to characterize this as a both-and approach. Wesley affirms the importance of both preaching and the sacraments. He affirms the importance of both corporate worship and small groups. He affirms the importance of both justification and sanctification. In this case, he affirms the importance of both faith and good works for salvation.

Two of Wesley's practices allow him to craft such delicately balanced positions. First, he has a very logical mind and pays strict attention to definitions and distinctions. We will see him discuss several senses of the word *necessary* as it applies to faith and works.

Second, his approach to biblical interpretation, as we saw in chapter 1, emphasizes the general tenor of the Bible—its whole message. He has a strong incentive to consider all of the places where salvation is discussed and look for a way to affirm the perspective contained in each text. All of his interpretative methods lead him to affirm both sides of any apparent biblical tension.

Wesley opens "The Scripture Way of Salvation" by remarking "How easy to be understood, how plain and simple a thing, is the genuine religion of Jesus Christ! Provided only that we take it in its native form, just as it is described in the oracles of God."[2] True religion for Wesley consists in salvation and faith, and he says it is "a plain and simple thing." He then proceeds to explain these terms in ways that may not strike most Christians as so simple.

During the new student orientation in Scott's first semester at Perkins School of Theology, the dean said something like the following: "In religion, there is simplicity, then complexity, and then simplicity again on the other side of complexity. As a leader in the church, you have no right to remain in the simplicity on this side of complexity. But you must also push through to the simplicity you will find after studying all of the complexity."[3] (He was warning the entering students about the difficulty of studying theology.) Wesley's simple answer about the nature of true religion is salvation by faith. But he then leads the reader into a complex description of those terms.

"For by grace you have been saved through faith, and this is not your own doing; it is the gift of God—not the result of works, so that no one may boast. For we are what he has made us, created in Christ Jesus for good works, which God prepared beforehand to be our way of life."
(Ephesians 2:8 NRSV)

The text for the sermon forms the basis for Wesley's both-and, simple-yet-complex position. Ephesians 2:8-10 reads: "For by grace you have been saved through faith, and this is not your own doing; it is the gift of God—not the result of works, so that no one may boast. For we are what he has made us, created in Christ Jesus for good works, which God prepared beforehand to be our way of life" (NRSV). Unlike the Romans 4 account that makes no mention of good works, here Paul says that human beings are intended by God to do good works as our way of life.

"The Scripture Way of Salvation" focuses on answering the questions, "What is salvation?" and "How does one obtain it?" Wesley starts off by clarifying that salvation is both a future and a present reality. His argument for this is the tense of the Greek verb in Ephesians 2:8. He is correct in noting that it could be translated as the present tense "you are saved" or the perfect tense "you have been saved." This leads to an important conclusion for Wesleyan Christians. Salvation is best understood, in Wesley's own words, as "the entire work of God, from the first dawning of grace in the soul till it is consummated in glory."[4] He specifically says that salvation thus includes God's "preventing" grace, which comes to us before we are aware of it.[5] Wesley cites John 1:9, which says that Christ is the light that enlightens everyone, as the proof of his teaching that all human beings are recipients of God's grace.

But in this sermon Wesley focuses on two main aspects of salvation. The first is called *justification*, which he defines as pardon. Because of Christ's death on the cross, human beings have the opportunity for their sins to be forgiven and they can be reconciled to God. Wesley describes this as a relative change, by which he means a change in the individual's relationship with God. A person who is justified is no longer separated from God because of sin but has been reconciled and accepted by God as one of God's children.

This change in relationship is fundamental to all that follows in the Christian life. If one is pardoned and is now in a right relationship with God, one assumes a new identity—a beloved child of God and member of God's family. One need not fear God's wrath or punishment, because the relationship is solid. This also includes reconciliation with the community of faith.

Yet, our God is a holy God with laws and expectations for how God's children should live. So in the very moment that we are justified, we also begin the process of sanctification. *Sanctification* as a word has the same root as *sanctuary*, from the Latin *sanctus* meaning "holy." While God's grace *pardons* us in justification, it *changes* us in sanctification. This is a real change, where our hearts are transformed and we become different persons.

> While God's grace pardons us in justification,
> it changes us in sanctification. This is a real
> change, where our hearts are transformed
> and we become different persons.

While justification is an instantaneous change in identity, sanctification is a process that takes the rest of our lives. We become more and more dead to sin and more and more alive to God. The power of sin in our lives decreases while the love of God and neighbor grows greater and greater. In a telling metaphor, Wesley describes religion as being like a house. Repentance is the porch, justification is the doorway, and sanctification is the rest of the house. Walking through the doorway gets us into the way of salvation, but we are then living that life for the rest of our days.

To the question, "How can I be saved," Wesley's answer is by faith. It is faith alone that is required for justification and sanctification. To define faith, he quotes Hebrews 11:1. He gives his own translation from the Greek, "a divine evidence and conviction of things not seen." For Wesley this is similar to turning on the light in a room. The reality of the room is already present in the darkness. When the light is turned on, one can see, understand, and be aware of what is truly there all along. If our physical eyes make us aware of the three-dimensional world, this spiritual sense makes us aware of the spiritual world. By faith we see that God is reconciling the world through Christ and offering salvation to everyone. More particularly, faith is the awareness that my own sins are forgiven and that Christ died for me. By this faith we receive Christ in all of his offices as prophet, priest, and king. Remembering that in the Greek of the New Testament the same word means "believe" and "have faith," we can say that when we believe we are saved. In this sense we are saved by faith alone.

Yet, in most circumstances, faith is never alone. Wesley's answer to the tension between faith and works is to acknowledge that good works are also in some sense necessary to salvation. But they are not necessary in the same way that faith is necessary.

Faith is necessary to salvation unconditionally. It is always and everywhere the fundamental requirement for both justification and sanctification. But good works are also required if there is time and opportunity. Good works are those actions whereby we obey God's law. Such works are necessary for genuine faith to continue and grow. Thus, Wesley can say that good works are conditionally necessary—that is, if there is time and opportunity. Wesley refers to the man crucified with Jesus who, as he was dying, acknowledged Jesus as the Messiah and was told, "I assure you that today you will be with me in paradise" (Luke 23:43). This man had faith, but no time or opportunity to obey God's commandments like feeding the hungry and giving water to the thirsty. Yet he was saved.

It is faith alone that saves us, but good works are necessary to continuing the life of faith.

It is also correct to say that good works are necessary to salvation indirectly. It is faith alone that saves us, but good works are necessary to continuing the life of faith. Here Wesley says that there are two kinds of good works: works of piety and works of mercy. Works of piety are the means of grace that connect us to God. Works of mercy are all the acts that exemplify our love of neighbor. We are called to do both.

Wesley acknowledges that when someone is justified, sanctification begins immediately. But we know that sin remains in the heart of the new Christian, and so there is a kind of repentance that is usually necessary even during the Christian's process of sanctification. While repentance normally means turning away from a life of sin and entering into the way of salvation, there is also a kind of repentance that is appropriate for believers as well. When a believer acknowledges some way in which he or she has fallen short of God's expectations, it is then an opportunity for God's grace to forgive that sin and help the believer not to do it again.

The Wesleyan Way of Salvation

Wesley's understanding of salvation is the best way of resolving the tensions in the Bible between faith and works. Two Scripture passages give a strong indication that he is on the right track. Ephesians 2:8-10, the main text of his sermon "The Scripture Way of Salvation," shows the balance Wesley is trying to strike:

> You are saved by God's grace because of your faith. This salvation is
> God's gift. It's not something you possessed. It's not something you
> did that you can be proud of. Instead, we are God's accomplishment,
> created in Christ Jesus to do good things. God planned for these good
> things to be the way that we live our lives.

Salvation is not something that one earns, and it is not the reward for doing a certain number of good works. It is a gift of grace that we receive by faith. Yet, that life of faith prepares us to do good things, which was God's plan for us all along.

Another key text shows the interplay between God's grace and our response. Philippians 2:12-13 says:

> Therefore, my loved ones, just as you always obey me, not just when I
> am present but now even more while I am away, carry out your own
> salvation with fear and trembling. God is the one who enables you both
> to want and to actually live out his good purposes.

Paul is here exhorting believers to obey the commandments and to carry out their own salvation. That sounds like human effort. But he then goes on to say that our human efforts are only possible because it is God working through us. That is the mystery of grace. We give God the glory for saving us. Yet, we know that, as St. Augustine said, the God who made us without ourselves will not save us without ourselves.

Salvation is a journey that includes all of God's work in the soul from the beginning to the end.

"How can I be saved?" Both Scripture and Wesley answer that salvation is a lifelong journey. When Christians sometimes talk about "getting saved" as if it were a one-time event, they are usually referring to an experience of being born again that is clearly identifiable as a specific movement when they were justified. Our Wesleyan approach certainly believes that such experiences are important and even necessary to the overall journey. But salvation is a journey that includes all of God's work in the soul from the beginning to the end.

And Can It Be that I Should Gain

John Wesley had his heart strangely warmed in a small group meeting on Aldersgate Street in London, May 24, 1738. His brother Charles had a similar experience three days earlier where he experienced saving faith in Christ. On the first anniversary of this experience, Charles wrote a hymn to describe what it was like.

And can it be that I should gain
an interest in the Savior's blood!
Died he for me? who caused his pain!
For me? who him to death pursued?
Amazing love! How can it be
that thou, my God, shouldst die for me?
Amazing love! How can it be
that thou, my God, shouldst die for me?

'Tis mystery all: th'Immortal dies!
Who can explore his strange design?
In vain the firstborn seraph tries
to sound the depths of love divine.
'Tis mercy all! Let earth adore;
let angel minds inquire no more.
'Tis mercy all! Let earth adore;
let angel minds inquire no more.

He left his Father's throne above
(so free, so infinite his grace!),
emptied himself of all but love,
and bled for Adam's helpless race.
'Tis mercy all, immense and free,
for O my God, it found out me!
'Tis mercy all, immense and free,
for O my God, it found out me!

Long my imprisoned spirit lay,
fast bound in sin and nature's night;
thine eye diffused a quickening ray;
I woke, the dungeon flamed with light;
my chains fell off, my heart was free,
I rose, went forth, and followed thee.
My chains fell off, my heart was free,
I rose, went forth, and followed thee.

No condemnation now I dread;
Jesus, and all in him, is mine;
alive in him, my living Head,
and clothed in righteousness divine,
bold I approach th'eternal throne,
and claim the crown, through Christ
my own.
Bold I approach th'eternal throne,
and claim the crown, through Christ
my own.[6]

3

Am I a Real Christian?

The Spiritual Question and Its Importance Today

Once someone has heard the message of the Bible and found salvation, what happens the next day at 8:00 a.m.? In chapter 2, we talked about salvation as both justification and sanctification—both a relative change and a real change—but what does that mean when the alarm goes off the next morning? One of Arthur's friends in high school attended a concert at his church where they offered people the opportunity to become a Christian. He accepted the offer, prayed, and became a Christian. Arthur and an adult leader took him to a side room to pray with him and talk about what happened. All he wanted to know is, "What do I do now?" You see, his parents weren't Christians and he knew that everything had changed, but he had never seen what a real, grown-up, complete Christian looked like. Unfortunately, for people seeking out examples, it is difficult to find out exactly what it means to be a "real" Christian.

Christians in the public sphere are often more confusing than helpful. Are Christians conservative or liberal? (Yes.) Are they Republicans or Democrats? (Yes.) If you were a new Christian (or a longtime Christian trying to become more serious about your faith) looking for a roadmap to follow, you would discover that the most visible Christians are pushing an agenda with which other Christians seem to disagree. How does a new believer—or anyone else for that matter—know what Jesus wants them to do? In the most extreme situations, this is more than confusing. It is damaging. When Arthur was a student at the University of Kansas, the most visible Christians seemed to be angry. They were holding up signs telling people they are going to hell. Other (well-meaning) Christians showed up simply to yell back. In this confusion, some decided that following Jesus meant deciding which type of Christian they did not want to be. Others rejected faith entirely, thinking, "If that is what a real Christian is, I want no part of Jesus."

The largest group of Christians in America isn't the conservative, or the liberal, or even the moderate Christians. The largest group is what we might call the **barely** Christian.

We believe, however, that the most damage that can be done to a new Christian isn't too much passion on one side or the other, but rather the lack of passion—an apathetic, indifferent faith. The largest group of Christians in America isn't the conservative, or the liberal, or even the moderate Christians. The largest group is what we might call the *barely* Christian. While the passionate and loud Christians get the public attention, the nominal Christians have the most negative impact. They are the ones who would send the message to Arthur's friend that nothing would need to change once he believed in Jesus. The greatest threat to Christianity is not the extremes, but the dead, apathetic, and indifferent center.

Kenda Creasy Dean wrote about this phenomenon in her book *Almost Christian: What the Faith of Our Teenagers Is Telling the American Church.* She drew upon data from the National Study of Youth and Religion, a massive research project studying the actual faith of American teenagers. The research uncovered that their faith was nothing like the Christian faith of the last two thousand years, but could be generally summarized as a minimal form of religion that Christian Smith, the director of the study, called Moralistic Therapeutic Deism (MTD). In an interview with ChurchLeaders.com, Dean summarizes MTD as follows: "Religion helps you to be nice (it's moralistic) and feel good (it's therapeutic), but otherwise God stays out of the way except in emergencies (it's Deist)."[1] The primary difference between MTD and full-blown agnostics is that agnostics are more honest about the fact that they believe faith to be irrelevant to their day-to-day lives. Kenda Creasy Dean discovered that our young people are articulating MTD because that is the way they see their parents actually live: it makes them feel better, but it doesn't challenge them or make them better people. Let's look at MTD as it would relate to Arthur's friend who received salvation and wants to know how to act the next morning at 8:00 a.m.

Moralistic. Be nice—that is, be a generally good person. Arthur's friend was already nice before he had found Jesus. He smiled to people in the hallways at school and didn't commit any horrible sins. According to MTD, he just needs to be the same person after he discovers Jesus that he was before that moment.

Therapeutic. Feel good. In her book, Dean calls this a self-serving spirituality.[2] It is a spirituality that requires nothing difficult or challenging. Consider Arthur's friend. He had been doing things that served himself his entire life. He was friends with people he wanted to be friends with and did things he wanted to do. Faith would only be there to make him feel good about what he was already doing; it asks nothing more of him.

Deist. An absent God. God, and therefore his faith, are irrelevant for Arthur's friend until he needs them. According to MTD, almost every day his faith is unused. Only in moments of true devastation or difficulty is God even remotely connected to his day-to-day experience, and even then it is a removed faith because it is a mostly absent God.

For too many people who claim to have a Christian faith, it is an almost Christianity rather than a real and complete Christianity. Is that a problem, though? In fact, it is. MTD seems so innocent, but sometimes the most seemingly harmless things can do the most damage. Consider a marriage where the couple is generally nice to each other, and no one ever does anything really bad, but it is otherwise lifeless. There is cordiality with no romance and deference with no passion. Indifference seems so harmless, but it will kill a marriage more surely than anger. We have done the same to our religion and to our world.

Elie Wiesel is a Jewish Holocaust survivor who received the Nobel Peace Prize and was a prolific writer. He is quoted as saying:

> The opposite of love is not hate, it's indifference. The opposite of art is not ugliness, it's indifference. The opposite of faith is not heresy, it's indifference. And the opposite of life is not death, it's indifference. Because of indifference, one dies before one actually dies.[3]

Today, Christianity is presented with a major difficulty because the most public forms of Christianity are hateful toward each other, and the most pervasive form of Christianity is weak and indifferent. Neither of these represents the faith described in Scripture, or the faith that we are called to live out. If neither of these is real Christianity, then what is? And more importantly, how can I know if I am a real Christian?

Today, Christianity is presented with a major difficulty because the most public forms of Christianity are hateful toward each other, and the most pervasive form of Christianity is weak and indifferent.

The Bible's Teaching

The Bible is a book about love. It is a complex book, but at its core it is about God and God is love. This is not an indifferent, detached, and insignificant love, but a deep, persistent, and overwhelming love. Love was present at the very creation of the world and at the engagement with Abraham and his descendants. It came into full reality in the person of Jesus. We Christians sometimes have made the error of ignoring the Old Testament in favor of Jesus, thinking that one is about love and the other is about rules. This is not the case—the Bible's teaching is about love cover to cover.

> The Bible is a book about love. It is a complex book,
> but at its core it is about God and God is love.

Pay attention to the Creation story. God created a garden and in it placed a human. God put good things in the garden—"the LORD God grew every beautiful tree with edible fruit" (Genesis 2:9)—and even paid attention to the human's personal well-being, noting that "it's not good that the human is alone. I will make him a helper that is perfect for him" (Genesis 2:18). From the very first moments God engaged with humanity, God was looking for ways to love God's creation.

That same expectation to love actively was placed upon the people of Israel in one of the most significant passages of the Law, Deuteronomy 6:4-5: "Israel, listen! Our God is the LORD! Only the LORD! Love the LORD your God with all your heart, all your being, and all your strength." Jesus later describes this as the first and greatest commandment, and points to another commandment in Leviticus 19:18 as the second greatest commandment, "you must love your neighbor as yourself; I am the LORD." Jesus wraps up his first and second greatest commands by saying that they are the theme by which you can understand everything, "All the Law and the Prophets depend on these two commands" (Matthew 22:37-40). Pay attention to the fact that the words *Law* and *Prophets* are capitalized here. In the Jewish world, those are important terms. The Law is comprised of the first five books of the Bible (Genesis, Exodus, Leviticus, Numbers, and Deuteronomy) and the Prophets are the Scriptures from prophets like Isaiah and Ezekiel that told the people of Israel what God wants. Jesus taught that all the commandments and stories of the Old Testament are summed up in the command to love God and love your neighbor.

The Ten Commandments are a perfect example of how Jesus' teaching helps us better understand Scripture. These commandments are the most famous of the Old Testament commandments and are highlighted in different places in Scripture. The Book of Exodus tells how Moses went to the top of a mountain to speak with God after the Israelites had been freed from Egypt. He came down with ten commandments on two tablets—the first four can be described as ways that we love God and the last six as ways that we love our neighbor. Tradition associates the first tablet with the commandments that center on loving God, and the second tablet with the ones centered on loving neighbor. Here is a summary of the commandments, which are listed in Exodus 20:1-17:

Tablet 1: Love God

1. "I am the LORD your God.... You must have no other gods before me."
2. "Do not make an idol for yourself."
3. "Do not use the LORD your God's name as if it were of no significance."
4. "Remember the Sabbath day and treat it as holy."

Tablet 2: Love Neighbor

5. "Honor your father and your mother."
6. "Do not kill."
7. "Do not commit adultery."
8. "Do not steal."
9. "Do not testify falsely against your neighbor."
10. "Do not desire your neighbor's house... wife, male or female servant, ox, donkey, or anything else that belongs to your neighbor."

Both tablets are crucial; we must love God and love our neighbors. The Ten Commandments are by no means a comprehensive list (as there are by tradition 613 commandments in the Old Testament), but they provide a framework for what it means to live and be faithful. Dr. J. Budziszewski, a professor at the University of Texas, has written about what he calls "The Second Tablet Project" where there is a strong modern tendency to want people to be nice to their neighbor (the second tablet), but to do it without believing in God (the first tablet).[4] His assessment of our culture is in line with what Kenda Creasy Dean found in her work, but the Bible knows nothing of such an exercise. The commandments of the Old and New Testaments say that these are interconnected ideas. You cannot love God without also loving your neighbor, and you cannot love your neighbor wholly unless you love God.

Jesus doubles down on the importance of fully living out both commandments. In the Gospel of Mark, immediately after Jesus' proclamation about the first and second greatest commandments, a dialogue begins with a legal expert:

The legal expert said to him, "Well said, Teacher. You have truthfully said that God is one and there is no other besides him. And to love God with all of the heart, a full understanding, and all of one's strength, and to love one's neighbor as oneself is much more important than all kinds of entirely burned offerings and sacrifices."

When Jesus saw that he had answered with wisdom, he said to him, "You aren't far from God's kingdom." After that, no one dared to ask him any more questions.

(Mark 12:32-34)

In our chapter on the Bible's message, we discussed that the basic message of Scripture was the kingdom of God. Jesus is telling us that fully loving God and loving our neighbor is how we attain and enact this Kingdom. It is more than just a list of dos and don'ts. It is about our hearts. Jesus, for instance, takes the seventh commandment (Do not commit adultery) and says that God hopes for more than outward behavior alone:

"You have heard that it was said, Don't commit adultery. But I say to you that every man who looks at a woman lustfully has already committed adultery in his heart. And if your right eye causes you to fall into sin, tear it out and throw it away. It's better that you lose a part of your body than that your whole body be thrown into hell. And if your right hand causes you to fall into sin, chop it off and throw it away. It's better that you lose a part of your body than that your whole body go into hell.

(Matthew 5:27-30)

Jesus' understanding of loving your neighbor is much more than anything our culture would say about "being nice" to someone else. Christianity as Jesus describes it is about a wholesale transformation of our heart, not just a lowest common denominator of decent action. Such a transformation is not possible without God.

> Christianity as Jesus describes it is about a wholesale transformation of our heart, not just a lowest common denominator of decent action. Such a transformation is not possible without God.

The early church knew that this high expectation of love was going to be difficult. When Paul is writing to Timothy, he writes that "the last days will be dangerous times. People will be selfish...unloving....They will look like they are religious but deny God's power. Avoid people like this" (2 Timothy 3:1-5). The Bible is not trying to get us to be people who merely go to church but rather to enact the kingdom of God with a radical love of both God and neighbor.

Wesley's Answer

Am I a real Christian? What is a real Christian anyway? Wesley's answer is to take Jesus seriously that fully loving God and loving neighbor is not only possible, but an expectation of a faithful Christian. Wesley's sermon "The Almost Christian" was written in 1741 but still applies today. Wesley's culture is not far from the one described by Kenda Creasy Dean. Eighteenth-century England was one where the formal church and the Christian universities had an outer appearance of faith and religiosity, but lacked the fervor of people whose hearts have been transformed. The sermon was given at Oxford University—a place where Wesley had received his own education and where he was a fellow of Lincoln College. Wesley gave a sermon about nominal Christianity in the heart of the place that he deemed full of nominal Christianity.

He begins by describing nominal Christianity as being "almost Christian." His focal text for the sermon is Acts 26:28, after Paul attempts to convert King Agrippa, where in the King James Version, Agrippa says, "Almost thou persuadest me to be a Christian." Wesley's decision to use this Scripture has less to do with Paul's attempt to convert Agrippa and more about the coining of the term "almost Christian." This sermon is not about non-Christians almost becoming Christians, but about Christians that lack an altogether faith.

He details what this almost-Christian life is like. Almost-Christians view doing evil the same as non-Christians—they generally avoid evil. They don't steal their neighbor's stuff or extort the poor or rich. Almost-Christians even go further than this—they do good. They give food to others, care for others, and basically follow the golden rule: "You should treat people in the same way that you want people to treat you" (Matthew 7:12). Wesley admits that almost-Christians even pay attention to the means of grace. This is a technical term for Wesley that refers to the ways that God gives God's grace to people, including through the sacraments. This means that an almost-Christian has been baptized, goes to church regularly, partakes of Holy Communion, and generally tries to do the things that God wants him or her to do.

An almost-Christian has been baptized, goes to church regularly, partakes of Holy Communion, and generally tries to do the things that God wants him or her to do.

You might be thinking, what is wrong with this? Isn't an almost-Christian a good thing? If everyone did these things, wouldn't the world be better? This is where Wesley's sermon takes a personal turn and we begin to understand that Wesley, like Jesus, presents a higher possibility. John Wesley publicly admits that he was the almost-Christian. For many years, he was "using diligence to [avoid] all evil, and to have a conscience void of offence...doing all good to all men; constantly and carefully using all the public and all the private means of grace." And yet, all of that wasn't enough. He says, "I was but 'almost a Christian.' "[5] The details of his life are clear enough to fill in the gaps in his sermon. During his time both at Oxford and as a preacher in Georgia, Wesley created communities whose purpose was to develop spiritual holiness. He was methodical (hence the term Methodist) at finding and following God, and yet he claims that he was merely an "almost-Christian."

His life changed on May 24, 1738 (three years before he delivered this sermon), when he was in a small group meeting on Aldersgate Street and the form of religion that he had followed became something more. He says that his heart was "strangely warmed." It was this experience that led him to lead the revival movement called Methodism. The sermon "The Almost Christian" describes his thoughts about what changes when you move (as he himself did) to being an altogether-Christian.

First, he says, we must love God. As is his standard practice, Wesley pulls in both the Old and New Testaments to highlight this transformation in which we truly come to love God. He quotes Isaiah 61:10, where the prophet says, "I will greatly rejoice in the LORD, my soul shall be joyful in my God" (KJV). He also quotes Mary in her response to discovering that she is to bear the Son of God; she says in Luke 1:47 that "my spirit hath rejoiced in God my Saviour" (KJV). Wesley connects this love of God, experienced as deep joy for Isaiah and Mary, with the death of our self-love as we, like Jesus, give up ourselves in order to love others. True joy in God is the death of our pride. It is a complete love of God, next to which we are "less than nothing in [our] own eyes."[6]

Second, Wesley says, we must love our neighbor. And if we, like the lawyer in Luke 10, ask who our neighbor is, we must understand that it is everyone in the world, even our enemies. We are to be like Jesus and love them as Christ loved us (John 13:34). This love that we have for others is to be pure and holy as described by 1 Corinthians 13. While we often use this passage to describe marriage, Wesley's understanding of loving our neighbor is that we ought to love all people, and that true love "puts up with all things, trusts in all things, hopes for all things, endures all things" (1 Corinthians 13:7).

Third, he says that we must have faith, as it says in John 3:16, "so that everyone who believes in him won't perish but will have eternal life." This is what Wesley himself found in his Aldersgate experience. Describing the event in his journal, he wrote, "I felt I did trust in Christ, Christ alone for salvation, and an assurance was given me that he had taken away *my* sins, even *mine*, and saved *me* from the law of sin and death."[7] This transformation is more than just a belief in God, or a belief that the Bible is true, or that the theology of the church is right. It is a faith that purifies the heart (James 4:8). It is a faith that fully loves God and fully loves neighbor, which means everyone.

---

*"I felt I did trust in Christ, Christ alone for salvation, and an assurance was given me that he had taken away **my** sins, even **mine**, and saved **me** from the law of sin and death."*

Wesley's answer about what it means to be a real Christian takes the Old and New Testament expectation of love seriously. The most powerful portion of his speech is that he personally knows what it is like to have the form of religion, but not have the power of love in his heart. This testimony is part of the power behind his message. He was preaching this message to the Oxford fellows in 1741, but also to us today who desire to live a Christlike life. He has a series of questions in the sermon to help you examine your heart. He writes:

> The great question of all, then, still remains. Is the love of God shed abroad in your heart? Can you cry out, "My God and my all"? Do you desire nothing but him? Are you happy in God? Is he your glory, your delight, your crown of rejoicing? And is this commandment written in your heart, "that he who loveth God love his brother also"? Do you then love your neighbour as yourself? Do you love every man, even your enemies, even the enemies of God as your own soul? As Christ loved you? Yea, dost thou believe that Christ loved *thee*, and gave himself for thee? Hast thou faith in his blood? Believest thou the Lamb of God hath taken away *thy* sins, and cast them as a stone into the depth of the sea? That he hath blotted out the handwriting that was against *thee*, taking it out of the way, nailing it to his cross? Hast *thou* indeed redemption through his blood, even the remission of *thy* sins. And doth his Spirit bear witness with *thy* spirit, that thou art a child of God?[8]

The Wesleyan Way of Salvation

Living an altogether Christian life is important both for us and for others. For us, it is important because it means that we live an authentic faith where our external and internal faith is congruent. It means that we no longer pretend to be religious while we are spiritually dead. Instead, we are transformed and live in such a way that the kingdom of God is made real here and now. It means we accept that God's gift of eternal life is available to us. For others, it is important because it means they have the opportunity to see Jesus displayed through others. Without altogether-Christians, they will have no other option but to believe that the weakened Christianity of our age is all that the Bible has to offer. Jesus' hope is that we would wake up each morning fully alive in our love of God, our love of neighbor, and our faith in God's salvation.

Jesus' hope is that we would wake up each morning fully alive in our love of God, our love of neighbor, and our faith in God's salvation.

This is what Arthur's friend should have been told when he asked what he was to do now that he was a Christian. He should have been told that when he wakes up the next morning, the kingdom of God is fully available to him. He can have a robust faith that fully loves God and loves neighbor. For many of us, that wholesale heart transformation doesn't always happen immediately. Wesleyans often talk about salvation as a process. Justification (as we talked about in the last chapter) is a moment, but sanctification often takes our whole lives. We are tempted to think that because sanctification is a process, the expectations of loving God and our neighbor are just something that happens *someday*—meaning that it can't happen *today*. This is not how Jesus talked about love or the kingdom of heaven. It is to happen now. Right now. And the next moment. And the moment after that. It is a process because we are still flawed. But if we expect less of ourselves, then we are accepting life as an almost-Christian.

> We are tempted to think that because sanctification is a process, the expectations of loving God and our neighbor are just something that happens someday—meaning that it can't happen today. This is not how Jesus talked about love or the kingdom of heaven. It is to happen now. Right now. And the next moment. And the moment after that.

It is like a marriage. If you are married, do you love your spouse every day? Completely love them? Love them so deeply that you would die for them? Sacrifice your own self? If you are like us, then your answer is probably, "I hope to be that person." We are hoping in every moment to do so. Do we always accomplish it? No, but there is a promise to expect that we will do it. Now take that same thought process to someone you perceive as an enemy. Do you love them? Completely love them? Love them so deeply that you would die for them? Sacrifice your own self? If you are like us then your answer is probably, "I don't really love them that way, but I want to love them that way."

Perhaps the greatest gift that Wesleyan Christianity has given to the Protestant Church is the emphasis that salvation is more than just for heaven. Salvation results in eternal life, but it begins now. It begins in our hearts, in the way we love both God and our neighbor. Salvation that doesn't include love of God and neighbor isn't salvation. Neither is it real Christianity. Like Jesus told Zacchaeus, may he also tell us: "Today, salvation has come to this household." May we be real Christians who love, truly love, God and neighbor.

Come, Let Us Use the Grace Divine

Charles Wesley's hymn "Come, Let Us Use the Grace Divine" is an encouragement for us to continually recommit our lives to God. We don't always succeed, but when we fail, we kneel, we ask for forgiveness. And we recommit our lives again to use the grace divine. It was traditionally used at the New Year in conjunction with the Covenant Prayer in the Wesleyan Tradition.

Come, let us use the grace divine,
and all with one accord,
in a perpetual covenant join
ourselves to Christ the Lord;
give up ourselves, thru Jesus' power,
his name to glorify;
and promise, in this sacred hour,
for God to live and die.

The covenant we this moment make
be ever kept in mind;
we will no more our God forsake,
or cast these words behind.
We never will throw off the fear
of God who hears our vow;
and if thou art well pleased to hear,
come down and meet us now

Thee, Father, Son, and Holy Ghost,
let all our hearts receive,
present with thy celestial host
the peaceful answer give;
to each covenant the blood apply
which takes our sins away,
and register our names on high
and keep us to that day![9]

4

Do I Have to Obey the Law?

The Spiritual Question and Its Importance Today

There are Christian churches that believe following Jesus is all about obedience to the rules. Members of such churches are taught a long list of things they must do and not do. Older and more senior members of the community are careful to teach "the rules" to new members and younger people. Such churches usually have clear and strong penalties for those who break the rules.

At the other end of the spectrum are those churches who believe that Christianity is all about grace and forgiveness. They focus on God's love and the fact that all human beings are sinners. They practice forgiveness and believe that penalties and punishments violate the law of love.

What is common to both of these situations is an either-or approach to the question of law and grace. When people think about the Bible's teaching on this matter, they sometimes go as far as saying that the Old Testament is a book of law and the New Testament is all about God's grace. Such an approach is superficial because God's laws and God's grace are found in both testaments. For the last 1,800 years, the Christian church has been unified in the acceptance of both the Old and the New Testaments.

God's laws and God's grace
are found in both testaments.

John Wesley, in establishing the new Methodist Episcopal Church in America in 1784, passed on an abbreviated version of the Church of England's Thirty-nine Articles of Religion (a set of basic doctrinal beliefs). One of those rules emphasized that the Old and the New Testaments are both preaching the same gospel, and the United Methodist doctrinal standards still include the following about the Old Testament:

> **Article VI—Of the Old Testament**
> The Old Testament is not contrary to the New; for both in the Old and New Testament everlasting life is offered to mankind by Christ, who is the only Mediator between God and man, being both God and Man. Wherefore they are not to be heard who feign that the old fathers did look only for transitory promises.[1]

While both testaments speak of both law and grace, there are two covenants, and the coming of Christ did change God's plan for the salvation of humankind.

There is a stronger emphasis on the function of the law in the Old Testament. This is understandable in the history of salvation, because God was choosing a people and forming them over time. As they left Egypt, they needed the Ten Commandments and other laws given on Mount Sinai. As they journeyed toward the Promised Land, God gave them civil laws to organize their life together as a people. God also gave them rules for how to worship and serve God. These laws shaped Israel as a distinct people, separated from other nations. Just as God is holy, they were called to be a holy people, set apart in a special relationship to the one God of Abraham.

The coming of Christ presumes all that has gone before, but adds a new emphasis on faith. The role of faith had always been present before in the Old Testament, but with the coming of Christ it takes on a new place. This became especially important as salvation was offered to the Gentiles, who had a different relationship to the law than did the Jews. In this way, grace is a stronger emphasis in the New Testament than the old.

Because both law and grace are offered throughout the Bible, which should we follow? Do we have to obey the law, or not? And what should the church do? Offer both rules and grace? A Wesleyan reading of the whole Scripture can help provide a way to do both.

The Bible's Teaching

When Jesus refers to the Old Testament, he describes it as "the Law and the Prophets." For example, when he is asked which commandment is the greatest (Matthew 22:36), he responds by quoting Deuteronomy 6:4-5 and Leviticus 19:18. He then says, "All the Law and the Prophets depend on these two commands" (Matthew 22:40). The third section of the Jewish Bible, called the Writings, did not take definitive shape as a category of Scripture until a century or so after Jesus' death and resurrection. The description of "the Law and the Prophets" shows the importance that the first five books of the Bible, the Law, held for the Jews at that time.

Jewish tradition holds that there are 613 commandments in the Law. Some are more important than others, which led to the question posed to Jesus in Matthew 22. Among the body of commandments, the Ten Commandments found in Exodus 20:1-17 held a special place. Yet, the rabbis sought to pay attention to all of the commandments so they would form a way of life for God's people. They became teachers and legal scholars, and they often disagreed with each other about how best to interpret the text of the Law.

These laws offered the Jewish people a way of salvation in the midst of a dangerous and chaotic world. There were multiple gods and religions among all of the peoples surrounding them, and following the law was a way for Jews to worship and to please the one true God. At the same time, the Lord was asking them to be God's people and to love God. At every point in the law, there was provision made for how to restore one's relationship to God when the laws are broken. The Book of Leviticus specifies a number of steps, including sacrifices and making restitution, that can be taken to obtain God's forgiveness and to restore the sinner back to a right relationship with the Lord. Just as rules for good conduct are specified, so are the methods of grace given as well.

An important part of Jewish history came with the prophets who were inspired by God to deliver messages to the people. While their messages sometimes addressed current events, other times they focused on the behavior of the people in light of God's will. Inevitably they interpreted the law by giving higher priority to some commandments over others. Some of them were very critical of the rituals that followed the law but neglected the more important matters. Consider Isaiah's words from his first chapter, verses 11-20:

> *What should I think about all your sacrifices?*
> *   says the LORD.*
> *I'm fed up with entirely burned offerings of rams*
> *   and the fat of well-fed beasts.*
> *   I don't want the blood of bulls, lambs, and goats.*
> *When you come to appear before me,*
> *   who asked this from you,*
> *   this trampling of my temple's courts?*
> *Stop bringing worthless offerings.*
> *   Your incense repulses me.*
> *New moon, sabbath, and the calling of an assembly—*
> *   I can't stand wickedness with celebration!*
> *I hate your new moons and your festivals.*
> *   They've become a burden that I'm tired of bearing.*
> *When you extend your hands,*
> *   I'll hide my eyes from you.*
> *Even when you pray for a long time,*
> *   I won't listen.*
> *Your hands are stained with blood.*
> *   Wash! Be clean!*
> *Remove your ugly deeds from my sight.*
> *   Put an end to such evil;*
> *   learn to do good.*
> *Seek justice:*
> *   help the oppressed;*
> *   defend the orphan;*
> *   plead for the widow.*

Come now, and let's settle this,
* says the LORD.*
Though your sins are like scarlet,
* they will be white as snow.*
If they are red as crimson,
* they will become like wool.*
If you agree and obey,
* you will eat the best food of the land.*
But if you refuse and rebel,
* you will be devoured by the sword.*
The LORD has said this.

Isaiah is appealing from one part of the law to another, more important part. He exaggerates God's dislike of ritual in favor of behaviors that address injustice and poverty. While demanding changed behavior, Isaiah also offers forgiveness for the people's sins.

"You have heard that it was said to those who lived long ago, **Don't commit murder,** and all who commit murder will be in danger of judgment. But I say to you that everyone who is angry with their brother or sister will be in danger of judgment."
(Matthew 5:21-22)

Jesus' preaching about the kingdom of God had strong similarities with the messages of the prophets. In the Sermon on the Mount, Jesus says, "Don't even begin to think that I have come to do away with the Law and the Prophets. I haven't come to do away with them but to fulfill them" (Matthew 5:17). Over the course of three chapters (Matthew 5–7), he then reinterprets the law saying that God expects us to meet a higher standard. For example, he says in 5:21-22, "You have heard that it was said to those who lived long ago, *Don't commit murder*, and all who commit murder will be in danger of judgment. But I say to you that everyone who is angry with their brother or sister will be in danger of judgment." Note that Jesus is quoting one of the Ten Commandments (Exodus 20:13) but then focusing on the interior character of the person in addition to the outward behavior. He does the same thing with adultery and lust in Matthew 5:27-28. When Jesus confronted the Pharisees, he accused them of paying too much attention to the least important parts of the law. But that did not mean they could forget about obeying even the smallest parts. He said:

> "How terrible it will be for you legal experts and Pharisees! Hypocrites! You give to God a tenth of mint, dill, and cumin, but you forget about the more important matters of the Law: justice, peace, and faith. You ought to give a tenth but without forgetting about those more important matters. You blind guides! You filter out an ant but swallow a camel."
>
> (Matthew 23:23-24)

At the same time, the Gospels record that Jesus offered grace and forgiveness to people. He healed people on the Sabbath. He ate dinner at the home of Zacchaeus, a notorious sinner. He spoke to the woman at the well breaking multiple rules in order to offer her living water. One of the best examples of him offering grace comes in the narrative in John 8:1-11. The legal experts brought to Jesus a woman caught in the act of adultery. They suggested stoning her to death. Jesus suggested that the first stone be thrown by the person who had not sinned. One by one the experts left. Jesus said to the woman, "Neither do I condemn you. Go, and from now on, don't sin anymore" (verse 11).

"Therefore, since we are justified
by faith, we have peace with God
through our Lord Jesus Christ."
(Romans 5:1 NRSV)

Paul's emphasis on salvation by grace continued Jesus' emphasis on forgiveness and including sinners and Gentiles. Paul was convinced that Christ's death and resurrection opened a way for Gentiles to be saved. Given his training as a rabbi, Paul originally thought that obedience to the law was required for salvation. His conversion and then the conversion of so many Gentiles led him to believe that salvation did not come from works of the law, but by faith. The Book of Romans contains an extended argument to prove that point. In chapter 2 above, we showed how Paul appeals to the example of Abraham. He says, "The promise to Abraham and to his descendants, that he would inherit the world, didn't come through the Law but through the righteousness that comes from faith" (Romans 4:13). This argument led Martin Luther and other Protestants to argue that we are saved by faith alone to emphasize our inability to earn salvation by doing good works. This clearly seems to be the message of Romans 5:1: "Therefore, since we are justified by faith, we have peace with God through our Lord Jesus Christ" (NRSV).

> "You see that a person is justified by works and not by faith alone."
>
> (James 2:24 NRSV)

The complexity of Scripture, however, is clearly illustrated by contrasting the message of James 2 with those verses in Romans. James also appeals to Abraham, but says that Abraham was justified because he offered his son Isaac on the altar. James concludes, "You see that a person is justified by works and not by faith alone" (James 2:24 NRSV).

A very important way to resolve this tension was determined by the apostles at the Jerusalem Council described in Acts 15. In chapter 1 above, we saw that the problem they faced was whether Gentile converts to Christianity were required to first become Jews with the requirement of obeying the law. Peter received a vision (described in Acts 10) that declared that what God had created as clean should not be called unclean. A Roman centurion named Cornelius sent for Peter that same day, and Peter responded to his vision by going to see Cornelius. While he was telling the household about Jesus, the Holy Spirit fell upon everyone who heard the word. Peter then said:

> "These people have received the Holy Spirit just as we have. Surely no one can stop them from being baptized with water, can they?" He directed that they be baptized in the name of Jesus Christ.
>
> *(Acts 10:47-48)*

Within the Christian community, Peter's decision was hotly debated. Paul was very much in favor of bringing Gentiles in. Finally, the apostles gathered in Jerusalem and concluded by sending a letter to all of the Christians. They said:

> The Holy Spirit has led us to the decision that no burden should be placed on you other than these essentials: refuse food offered to idols, blood, the meat from strangled animals, and sexual immorality. You will do well to avoid such things.
>
> *(Acts 15:28-29)*

Over time, this came to be understood as distinguishing three types of law in the Old Testament: ceremonial, civil, and moral. The Jerusalem Council's decision eventually came to mean that all of the commandments having to do with ceremonies and civil matters were not binding on Gentiles who became Christians. All of the moral commandments, however, such as sexual immorality and food offered to idols, were binding on Christians.

Wesley's Answer

The distinction between the three types of law is crucial to the background of Wesley's answer about how we should understand the role of the law in Christian life. We have seen Wesley's affirmation of the Thirty-Nine Articles of the Church of England. Article VI quoted above continues and explicitly refers to the three-way distinction about the commandments in the Old Testament:

> Although the law given from God by Moses as touching ceremonies and rites doth not bind Christians, nor ought the civil precepts thereof of necessity be received in any commonwealth; yet notwithstanding, no Christian whatsoever is free from the obedience of the commandments which are called moral.[2]

Nowhere is an authoritative list given, either in the teachings of the Church of England or in Wesley's writings, of which commandments fall into which category. However, when talking about how Christians should relate to the law, Wesley has in mind that it is only the moral law we should be concerned about.

In his two sermons "The Law Established Through Faith, I and II" Wesley makes explicit reference to the distinction. Both sermons work from Romans 3:31, which reads in the King James Version, "Do we then make void the law through faith? God forbid: yea, we establish the law." The Common English Bible renders it as, "Do we then cancel the Law through this faith? Absolutely not! Instead, we confirm the Law." Wesley makes it very clear that the law we are establishing or confirming is the moral law.

The moral law is an essential part of Wesley's understanding of God. In a related sermon, Wesley quotes Romans 7:12, "So the Law itself is holy, and the commandment is holy, righteous, and good." Wesley knows that God is love, and that the law is important as a revelation of who God is. He says, "It is the face of God unveiled; God manifested to his creatures as they are able to bear it; manifested to give and not to destroy life; that they may see God and live. It is the heart of God disclosed to man."[3] He believes that the law is "supreme unchangeable reason" and "a copy of the eternal mind."[4]

> Like a physician who sees beyond
> our pain to the underlying disease, the law
> tells us what is really going wrong in our lives.

For these reasons, Christianity upholds the law precisely because it is holy, just, and good. These three characteristics are manifested by the three uses by which the law functions in the way of salvation. First, the law convinces us of sin. It is sharper than any two-edged sword (Hebrews 4:12). The law exposes a person's real condition and strips away all of our self-deceptions and illusions. We see ourselves as we really are, standing guilty before God. It is the law that convinces us that we, in reality, lack spiritual life and are dead in our sins. Oftentimes people have a vague sense that something is wrong in their lives without being able to describe it exactly. Maybe there is unresolved conflict in one's family, or self-destructive behavior, or a loss of meaning and direction. In such circumstances, the law provides a diagnosis of what is wrong. Like a physician who sees beyond our pain to the underlying disease, the law tells us what is really going wrong in our lives.

The second use of the law is to bring us to life in Christ. The law is like a severe schoolmaster who brings us to know Christ even if the process is painful. The law not only provides a diagnosis, but it points to the solution—how to focus our lives on the grace of Jesus Christ as the answer to our problems.

The third use of the law is to keep us alive. Once we know the disease and once we know Christ as the healer, the law then teaches us how to live in obedience to Christ. For Wesley, this is the controversial part because some people believe that Christians are freed from the law and are under grace. They can quote Romans 10:4, which in the King James Version says, "Christ is the end of the law for righteousness to every one that believeth." But the word translated as "end" could equally be translated as "goal" and so the Common English Bible for that same verse reads, "Christ is the goal of the Law, which leads to righteousness for all who have faith in God." Wesley believes that sin still remains in our hearts after we accept Christ as our Savior and that the law reminds us of the ways in which we still fall short of God's expectations. The law has as its purpose to continually draw us closer to Christ both before we accept him (the second use of the law) and after we accept him (the third use of the law).

How does this emphasis on the uses of the law fit with Wesley's emphasis on grace? Scott has described Wesley's theological position as "the extreme center." He sees Wesley as holding in tension important parts of the Christian faith that often are seen as contradictory. Wesley's dual emphasis on both grace and the law is typical of this approach. He explains his interpretation of Scripture in the sermon "Upon Our Lord's Sermon on the Mount, V." Wesley is trying to explain the meaning of Matthew 5:18, "Till heaven and earth pass, one jot or one tittle shall in no wise pass from the law, till all be fulfilled" (KJV). He writes,

From all this we may learn that there is no contrariety at all between the law and the gospel; that there is no need for the law to pass away in order to the establishing of the gospel. Indeed, neither of them supersedes the other, but they agree perfectly well together. Yea, the very same words, considered in different respects, are parts of the law and of the gospel. If they are considered as commandments, they are parts of the law: if as promises, of the gospel. Thus, "Thou shalt love the Lord thy God with all thy heart," when considered as a commandment, is a branch of the law; when regarded as a promise, is an essential part of the gospel—the gospel being no other than the commands of the law proposed by way of promises. Accordingly, poverty of spirit, purity of heart, and whatever else is enjoined in the holy law of God, are no other, when viewed in a gospel light, than so many great and precious promises....

We may yet farther observe that every command in Holy Writ is only a covered promise.[5]

Wesley's solution to the superficial opposition of grace and the law is faithful to Scripture. On the one hand, it requires that believers go deeper into their understanding of exactly what is grace and what is the law. Far too many of the debates in the Christian community can be settled if people would just think more deeply about what each of them means. On the other hand, there are key texts that show that both are important and somehow must be held together. One such text is Ephesians 2:8-10, which says:

For by grace you have been saved through faith, and this is not your own doing; it is the gift of God—not the result of works, so that no one may boast. For we are what he has made us, created in Christ Jesus for good works, which God prepared beforehand to be our way of life.

(NRSV)

Paul is clear that salvation is by grace through faith, but the result of this salvation is that the Christian will do good works. We are not saved *by* good works—we are saved *for* good works. Wesley also was fond of using Philippians 2:12-13, where Paul urges believers to work out their own salvation, because it is God who is working in them and enabling them to work.

We are not saved by good works—
we are saved for good works.

When considered carefully, God's saving activity and our faithful work in response all fit together without contradiction and in complete harmony with Scripture.

For these reasons, Wesley argues that we are to "establish" the law. He suggests that we do this in three ways. First we are to establish the law by our teaching. Leaders of the church, whether pastors or laity, need to understand how the law and grace fit together and are not contradictory. We then need to teach new believers about it. We need to explain the difference between commandments in the Old Testament that are no longer binding and those that are still applicable for us to please God.

Wesley also distinguishes between the literal sense and the spiritual sense. We are to teach obedience to the literal sense of the commandments (that is, the moral law), but also pay attention to the spiritual sense as well. By the spiritual meaning he wants people to teach the inward principles that relate to "the thoughts, desires, and intents of the heart."[6]

Secondly, we establish the law when we teach the kind of faith that produces holiness. He writes that "love is the end of all the commandments of God."[7] When a comparison is made, love is always more important than faith. Wesley speculates that the angels before creation had no need of faith since they saw God face to face, but they did have a need for love. Prior to Adam's sin, there was no need for faith by him, but there was a place for love. Faith was needed only after the first sin. Wesley says:

> And it was only when love was lost by sin that faith was added, not for its own sake, nor with any design that it should exist any longer than until it had answered the end for which it was ordained— namely, to restore man to the love from which he was fallen....

> Faith then was originally designed of God to re-establish the law of love. Therefore, in speaking thus, we are not undervaluing it, or robbing it of its due praise, but on the contrary showing its real worth, exalting it in its just proportion, and giving it that very

place which the wisdom of God assigned it from the beginning. It is the grand means of restoring that holy love wherein man was originally created.[8]

Reading this subordination of faith to love calls to mind the closing verse of 1 Corinthians 13, "Now faith, hope, and love remain—these three things—and the greatest of these is love" (verse 13).

The third and most important way in which Christians establish the law is by establishing it in our own hearts and lives. If we do not walk the walk, all the talking is useless. Wesley puts it bluntly:

> And yet, all this time, if the law we preached were not established in our hearts we should be of no more account before God than "sounding brass or tinkling cymbals." All our preaching would be so far from profiting ourselves that it would only increase our damnation.[9]

The solution for how to do this is faith. It is only by faith that we can make progress toward holiness. If we are focused on God and God's will for our lives, it is easy and natural to do what God has commanded. The knowledge that God has loved us and forgiven our sins through the death of Christ naturally leads us to love God back and to love our neighbor as ourselves.

If we are focused on God and God's will for our lives, it is easy and natural to do what God has commanded.

The Wesleyan Way of Salvation

We take the Bible very seriously, and we are seeking to obey the moral law. We cannot follow Jesus and simply ignore his words as if they were meant for other people in a different time. There are days when each of us, both Scott and Arthur, has been driven to our knees saying, "O God, I cannot do this. You are asking more than I can deliver. I am just not able to live by your expectations." That is when God reminds us that we are saved by grace through faith, and that salvation is a journey on which believers travel for their whole lives.

When salvation is seen as a lifelong process with distinct stages, the role of the law becomes clear. Let's remember the way of salvation in general:

- Creation in the image of God.
- Sin (brokenness)
- Repentance (turning back to God)
- Justification (returning to relationship with God)
- Sanctification (becoming holy and restoring the image of God)

At each stage of the process, grace comes to the believer. Prevenient grace is at work before anyone is aware of it. Convincing grace helps us know our sinfulness and our need for God, leading us toward repentance. Justifying grace pardons our sins and changes our relationship with God. Sanctifying grace helps us go on to Christian maturity.

But there is a role for the law at every stage but one as well. Wesley believes that conscience or the ability to distinguish between right and wrong is not natural; rather, it is a supernatural gift of God to every human being. This is the dim awareness that all human beings have of God's laws. The awareness of sin and the drive to repent are a direct result of hearing God's laws and knowing how far we have fallen short. This is what brings us to Christ. Once we are justified, it is the law that keeps us alive by teaching us how to make further progress toward God's goal for our lives.

While God's grace is present at every stage, it is only at the place of justification where there is no role for the law. If we think of salvation as a house, justification is the moment we walk through the door and enter. The law can take us to the porch where we repent, but becoming a Christian has nothing to do with the law—it is all by the gift of God. No one stands in the doorway forever. It is an instantaneous change in our relationship with God, and we move on to live in the house where, as in every house, there are rules. Wesley is clear that the goal of the Christian life is entire sanctification or perfection.

Perfection for Wesley is that state where all of our thoughts, words, and deeds are motivated by love of God and love of neighbor. It is not sinless because we will make mistakes and break God's laws unintentionally. But it is possible to reach a place (even if it is on our deathbed in our last moments) when our hearts are pure and we love God fully.

Wesley translated the New Testament and wrote comments on the verses. His *Explanatory Notes Upon the New Testament* remains a doctrinal standard for The United Methodist Church. While he followed the King James Version most of the time, there are notable exceptions. The KJV for Matthew 5:48 reads, "Be ye therefore perfect, even as your Father which is in heaven is perfect." Wesley's translation is different: "Therefore ye shall be perfect, as your Father who is in heaven is perfect." He comments,

> So the original runs, referring to all that holiness which is described in the foregoing verses, which our Lord in the beginning of the chapter recommends as happiness, and in the close of it as perfection.
>
> And how wise and gracious is this, to sum up, and, as it were, seal all his commandments with a promise! Even the proper promise of the Gospel! That he will *put* those *laws in our minds, and write them in our hearts!* He well knew how ready our unbelief would be to cry out, this is impossible! And therefore stakes upon it all the power, truth, and faithfulness of him to whom all things are possible.[10]

Both of us were asked by our bishop at the time of our ordination, "Are you going on to perfection?" and "Do you expect to be made perfect in love in this life?" We said yes to both questions. But anyone who wants to hold us accountable for those answers should recognize that the questions are not just for clergy. They apply to all Christians, and therefore guide how our churches should operate. Every church should offer unlimited grace and love, but knowing that perfection is the goal for all of us, it must also lift up God's moral law as a standard we strive to achieve. Like Wesley, we hold to both the law and grace; we seek to shape our hearts, minds, and behavior to love God fully and love our neighbors as ourselves.

We hold to both the law and grace; we seek to shape our hearts, minds, and behavior to love God fully and love our neighbors as ourselves.

A Charge to Keep I Have

Charles Wesley's hymn "A Charge to Keep I Have" is his acknowledgment that obedience to the moral law is important. Yet it is a prayer to God for the power to do what God has commanded, knowing that is the only way to fulfill God's desires.

A charge to keep I have,
a God to glorify,
a never-dying soul to save,
and fit it for the sky.

To serve the present age,
my calling to fulfill;
O may it all my powers engage
to do my Master's will!

Arm me with jealous care,
as in thy sight to live,
and oh, thy servant, Lord, prepare
a strict account to give!

Help me to watch and pray,
and on thyself rely,
assured, if I my trust betray,
I shall forever die.[11]

5

Am I a Sinner?

The Spiritual Question and Its Importance Today

A number of years ago at Arthur's church, two young women were debriefing the sermon as they walked down the hallway, unaware that they were being overheard. One said to the other, "I hate it when they talk about sin; it is such a downer!" This is not just a sentiment shared by young people. In a different church that we have served, a husband and father complained about the parts of the service that included confessing our sins. This man wanted what those young women seemed to want: a focus on positive messages while avoiding "downers" like brokenness and sin. This man, it turns out, ended up leaving his wife and children due to an affair with his secretary. It isn't that we aren't broken; we simply do not like to be reminded of it. We want to feel good! And yet, as this example shows, it's important to confront the reality that sin lies within every person. We all have a tendency to seek our own interests and turn away from love of God and neighbor. It does us no good to pretend otherwise.

When Arthur was growing up, there was an entire approach to raising and teaching children that emphasized self-esteem, making sure that children focus on the positive aspects of themselves. This movement was made popular by a best-selling book entitled *The Psychology of Self-Esteem*, written by Nathaniel Branden. This is one reason everyone who participated in some sporting events got trophies: no child had to go home as a loser.

Despite its positive outcomes, this movement's heavy emphasis on affirmation and esteem resulted in at least one generation of children (called millennials) being raised to minimize loss and potentially ignore their weaknesses. Now, don't get us wrong. We aren't saying that the effort to focus on self-worth, or esteem, is bad. Children absolutely need to know that they have value and are loved. The problem comes when this message of value and love becomes distorted to give us an unrealistic picture of the world's difficulties or our own capacity to fail and act wrongfully.

Unfortunately, that distortion happens all too easily and often. What happens to those children when they grow up and realize that the world is not as positive as they've been led to expect? What happens to those children when they grow up and realize that loss is inevitable for everyone at some point? If you search online for "participation trophies," you can find opinion pieces with titles like "Participation Trophies Are the Worst Thing You Can Give a Kid"[1] and "Participation Trophies Send a Dangerous Message."[2] These essays aren't scientific studies, but they are testimonies of people who have come to believe that the self-worth process did not prepare them or their peers for the real world.

In contrast, consider the wiser and more balanced perspective taught by a beloved children's TV host, the singing, cardigan-wearing, ordained Presbyterian minister named Mr. Rogers. His opening song says, "I like you just the way you are!" This sentiment sounds a lot like a participation trophy. But a closer look reveals that he paired this message with an acknowledgment of how people can fail. He helped children understand how to respond when they do bad things, or when bad things happen around them. Admittedly, Arthur has a soft spot for Mr. Rogers as it was one of the only shows that he and his siblings were allowed to watch. But what Mr. Rogers suggested by his words and attitude is a much wiser idea than the average pop-psychology movement about self-worth, precisely because of his faith. His love and compassion for others is influenced by what he understood God's message to be: everyone is loved and everyone is valued. This is at the very core of the Christian faith, but it is not the entirety of the Christian faith. Mr. Rogers knew that while we are always of infinite worth, we are not always who we ought to be. It was for this reason that he talked about the need to share, and what to do with mad feelings, and what to do when things are hard. He knew that we are not always who we ought to be, but that our worst moments don't decrease our value.

The faith of Mr. Rogers stands in this tension between the worth and value that we have and the brokenness in which we live. In an interview, the author of a book on Mr. Rogers entitled *Peaceful Neighbor* says, "It doesn't take a great leap to see Rogers as a saint. He was so patient and compassionate and accepting. But Rogers himself was aware that all of us are morally complex, a beautiful combination of saint and sinner."[3] This was highlighted recently in an online meme shared widely on the Internet that shows a classic picture of Mr. Rogers in a bright red cardigan with words superimposed that say, "You are not acting like the person Mr. Rogers knew you could be." Mr. Rogers' brilliance was his way of acknowledging that we are of immense worth, but that we can also be lonely, sad, angry, and broken.

When Scott was teaching classes about theology, he always told the story of Arthur and his twin sister Marynell. The question Scott would ask his students was, "How many pacifiers are necessary for twins?" The seemingly obvious answer is two, one for each mouth. The real answer, though, is six: one for each mouth and one for each hand. If they had a single hand free, they would grab the pacifier from their sibling's mouth and make her or him cry. From the earliest moment Arthur and his sister existed, they enjoyed taking things from their brother or sister and making them angry. This is sin. This is evidence of brokenness as a fundamental part of being human. Brené Brown is a research professor in the area of social work who has become famous for her talks on courage and vulnerability. She says in a TED Talk,

> Let me tell you what we think about children: they are hardwired for struggle when they get here. When you hold those perfect little babies in your hand, our job is not to say, "Look at her. She's perfect. My job is just to keep her perfect, make sure she makes the tennis team by fifth grade and Yale by seventh grade." That's not our job. Our job is to look and say, "You know what, you're imperfect, and you are wired for struggle, but you are worthy of love and belonging." That's our job.[4]

It turns out that starting from a place that accepts our brokenness and our limitations is actually the starting point of wisdom. "Am I a sinner?" Yes, I am. You are. We all are. But acknowledging our brokenness isn't a "downer" as the girl from Arthur's church said; rather, it is reality—as is the grace that God offers to heal us.

The Bible's Teaching

The reality of our brokenness is a story told on almost every page of the Bible. Only the first two chapters of Genesis and the last two chapters of Revelation describe a world that is free from brokenness and sin. In the first chapter of Genesis, God creates the entire world, including human beings. It only takes the first humans three chapters to eat the fruit from the only forbidden tree, then realize that they are naked and should hide from God. Adam blames Eve, Eve blames the snake, and before we are four chapters into the Bible, humanity has been kicked out of paradise. In just the fourth chapter, Adam and Eve's son Cain murders his brother Abel. This is hardly an auspicious beginning for humans on earth.

The reality of our brokenness is a story told on almost every page of the Bible.

The Bible then describes the spread of humanity over the face of the earth, but this is a broken and sinful group. In Genesis 6, it describes humanity from God's perspective: "The LORD saw that humanity had become thoroughly evil on the earth and that every idea their minds thought up was always completely evil" (Genesis 6:5). All are evil except for Noah and his family, so God decided to start over with the exception of this one family. God sent a flood to wipe out all life, but instructed Noah to build a boat to save himself, his family, and two of every kind of animal. The crucial point to this story is not merely the brokenness and sinfulness of humans (which didn't end with the Flood), but rather the end of the story where God promises that he is never going to flood the earth again. God places a rainbow in the sky and makes a covenant with humanity. The brokenness isn't gone from humans after the Flood, but God develops another approach.

God's new way of engaging humanity revealed itself in his relationship with a man by the name of Abraham. God makes a covenant with him personally and says that all of the people of the earth will be blessed because of his family (Genesis 12:3). God began working with Abraham and his descendants like Isaac, Jacob, and later Moses, giving them a series of rules and guidelines to guide them in maintaining right relationships with one another and with God. These included circumcision, avoiding the worship of idols, the appropriate ways to worship God, the clothes they should wear, and the food that they eat. These rules formed the basis of the covenant between God and the Israelites, setting the goal of purity and holiness. This is not a goal that the Israelites fully lived into; like the rest of humanity, the Israelites fell short.

The great difficulty of sin is that it is never far from humanity— even in the best families or the best people.

Much of the Old Testament shows the ways the Israelites fell short. When they were in the wilderness, they lost faith and began worshiping false idols. They refused to go into the Promised Land because it seemed too dangerous and difficult, even suggesting that they should return to slavery in Egypt rather than follow God. There were faithful individuals and moments where the whole people were faithful, but the general feeling in reading the stories of the Israelites is that wherever humans are, sin and brokenness are not far behind. One example is the high priest Eli as described in the beginning chapters of 1 Samuel. Eli was a faithful leader trying to do the right thing, but his sons were "despicable men who didn't know the LORD" (1 Samuel 2:12). They stole from the offerings of God and had sex with women who were off limits. Because of their corrupt leadership, the ark of the covenant that contained the laws passed down by Moses ended up captured by their enemies. The great difficulty of sin is that it is never far from humanity—even in the best families or the best people.

King David, for instance, was the best that the Israelites had to offer. He was the one with the courage to fight the giant Goliath because of his great faith in God. Due to his faithfulness and the fact that he had a heart like God's own (1 Samuel 13:14 NRSV), he became king over Israel. Yet even this man—the best Israel had to offer—got dragged down by his own sin. While on his rooftop, David saw a woman bathing. He summoned her to his palace and had sex with her. When she became pregnant, he arranged for her husband to be killed to cover it up (2 Samuel 11). The prophet Nathan called him out for his sin and David repented (2 Samuel 12), but it is a crucial part of Scripture that even the best of humanity fails to live up to the holiness that God seeks for us. Later kings were not even as good as King David. The kings of Judah were descended from David, but with only a few exceptions they are described in the Bible like this: "He did what was evil in the LORD's eyes, just as all his ancestors had done" (2 Kings 23:32).

In the New Testament, we see the brokenness continue, not just in the hearts of Jesus' detractors, but even among Jesus' closest friends and disciples. Judas ends up betraying Jesus, and Thomas doubts Jesus' resurrection. Even Peter (the first pope and leader of the Christian church) denied Jesus three times, and in another instance Jesus called him out as Satan. Paul, the greatest evangelist of the church, describes himself in the Book of Romans like this: "Instead, it's sin that lives in me. I know that good doesn't live in me—that is, in my body. The desire to do good is inside of me, but I can't do it. I don't do the good that I want to do, but I do the evil that I don't want to do" (Romans 7:17-19). Earlier in Romans, he sums up the brokenness of humanity simply and directly: "All have sinned and fall short of God's glory" (Romans 3:23). An understanding of sin is essential to a complete understanding of either ourselves or Scripture, but while it permeates our lives and almost every page of the Bible, sin does not have the final word.

Jesus entered into this world that had been sinful since almost the very beginning, but he came to provide forgiveness, healing, and love—which is called grace. In the ninth chapter of Matthew, some friends bring a paralyzed man to Jesus, and the Bible says, "When Jesus saw their faith, he said to the man who was paralyzed, 'Be encouraged, my child, your sins are forgiven'" (Matthew 9:2). Jesus later heals the man's body so that he can walk again, but notice that the first thing that Jesus does is to forgive his sins! Jesus came to fulfill the work that God began with Abraham many centuries earlier; the sin and brokenness that we all live in is not something that is to reign forever. Jesus came to offer us this grace, and the offer spread not just to the descendants of Abraham but to the entire world. Acts 15 tells of the first council of the church where Peter stands up and explains what God has done: "We believe that we and they are saved in the same way, by the grace of the Lord Jesus" (Acts 15:11).

Jesus' resurrection is the promise that the brokenness in our world—sin and its consequence, death—will be healed. In his chapter on the Resurrection, Paul writes in 1 Corinthians 15:

> *Death has been swallowed up by a victory.*
> *Where is your victory, Death?*
> *Where is your sting, Death?*
>
> *(Death's sting is sin, and the power of sin is the Law.) Thanks be to God,*
> *who gives us this victory through our Lord Jesus Christ!*
> *(1 Corinthians 15:54b-57)*

The completion of this victory is described in the last two chapters of Revelation, where the world once again resembles the paradise God intended in Genesis 1 and 2:

> *I heard a loud voice from the throne say, "Look! God's dwelling is here*
> *with humankind. He will dwell with them, and they will be his peoples.*
> *God himself will be with them as their God. He will wipe away every*
> *tear from their eyes. Death will be no more. There will be no mourning,*
> *crying, or pain anymore, for the former things have passed away."*
> *(Revelation 21:3-4)*

The promise of Scripture is that Jesus' work—his life, death, and resurrection—offers us the grace that heals us from our sins now and finally in the end of all things. Sin and brokenness are crucial to understanding Scripture and our lives, but in the end grace wins.

Sin and brokenness are crucial to understanding Scripture and our lives, but in the end grace wins.

Wesley's Answer

John Wesley did not underestimate sin; in fact, he believed that the reality of sin and brokenness is obvious in our world. The Scripture that he used in his sermon "Original Sin" comes from the opening to the story of Noah: "every idea their minds thought up was always completely evil" (Genesis 6:5). Wesley emphasizes that the reality of sin is a consistent message of the Scriptures, saying that "the same account is given by all the apostles, yea, by the whole tenor of the oracles of God."[5] Reading Scripture with Wesley requires that we pay close attention to themes that are repeated throughout Scripture and that are evident with the experience of our own lives, like the pervasiveness of sin. In Wesley's experience, the default position of the human heart is not to love God or to be selfless, but to do whatever we wish to do and whatever brings us pleasure. In this, he says that all men are "atheists in the world"[6] and that we operate in a cycle of pride and self-will where Satan and we work together to love the world and desire the flesh. In an especially strong assessment of human nature, he says that the human "with all his good breeding and other accomplishments, has no pre-eminence over the goat."[7]

If we are all broken and sinful, it means that each of us can dismiss pride and self-glory over another person because this sinful nature is true of all of us.

If this seems a particularly bleak assessment of humanity, it becomes the place where wisdom and hope are provided. If we are all broken and sinful, it means that each of us can dismiss pride and self-glory over another person because this sinful nature is true of all of us. Which of us, Wesley asks, hasn't lusted? hasn't had pride? He pulls from the rhetoric of Jesus in the eighth chapter of John, when a woman caught in adultery is about to be stoned. Jesus looks at the angry crowd and calms them down by saying, "Whoever hasn't sinned should throw the first stone" (John 8:7). Wesley asks us the same question, undercutting condemnation from any human source because sin affects every human at the core. The concept of original sin, rather than something depressing, becomes the foundation of Christian wisdom. Non-Christians and Christians alike agree that there is vice and brokenness in our world, but Wesley sees this concept as a dividing line separating true Christianity from everything else. He writes:

> Is man by nature filled with all manner of evil? Is he void of all good? Is he wholly fallen? Is his soul totally corrupted? Or, to come back to the text, is "every imagination of the thoughts of his heart evil continually"? Allow this, and you are so far a Christian. Deny it, and you are but a heathen still."[8]

Proper religion is an acknowledgment that we are so broken and diseased that we cannot heal ourselves. The danger in thinking that we are partially broken is that we might not fully submit to God, desiring to hold on to some part of this world. We must know that we are beyond our own help.

This would, indeed, be a difficult message if we were left to our own devices, but Scripture does not end here. It ends not with brokenness, but with healing. If our world is as broken as Scripture and our experience tell us, then it requires healing that cannot come from ourselves. Jesus is the great physician who came to reverse our brokenness, "to heal this sickness; to restore human nature, totally corrupted in all its faculties." We do this by knowing God—by ceasing to be atheists through knowing Jesus and his love. Since we cannot do this on our own, it is simply by grace—the gift of healing and forgiveness from God. All we can do is to accept the gift.

"Am I a sinner?" The Christian answer is yes, because we all are. Yet in Wesley's writings, the concept of original sin is not depressing, but a gift! Trying to hold on to some part of ourselves—claiming any part as completely good or holy—is to hold on to some element of our pride, or our self-centeredness, or our love of the world. This is what Wesley says "heathens" or "atheists" do, and what it does is keep us from fully accepting and living into the grace of God. We Christians like to think of grace as the greatest concept of the Christian faith. In the idea of original sin, Wesley reminds us of the context of God's grace through Jesus Christ: it came about because of our tendency to turn away from God. In our total corruption, we find hope. "By nature ye are wholly corrupted; by grace ye shall be wholly renewed.... Now 'go on' 'from faith to faith,' until your whole sickness be healed, and all that 'mind be in you which was also in Christ Jesus'!"[10]

The Wesleyan Way of Salvation

As we have seen in each of these chapters, the Wesleyan approach to salvation is more than just a single moment of transformation. We began with the concept that Scripture calls us to expect both a relative change (justification) and a real change (sanctification) in our lives. Wesley's understanding of Jesus as a physician helps us understand our reliance upon God. It is a unifying image, bringing together justification and sanctification. Jesus as the physician not only forgives our sins, but also heals our broken nature. We can be forgiven, but forgiveness is a gift from God. Likewise, we can be healed and made holy, but this healing is also a gift from God.

Jesus as the physician not only forgives our sins, but also heals our broken nature.

In order to receive this gift of God's grace, we are required to let go of everything, including our pride and our self-will. C. S. Lewis, in his preface to *The Great Divorce*, writes, "If we insist on keeping Hell (or even Earth) we shall not see Heaven: if we accept Heaven we shall not be able to retain even the smallest and most intimate souvenirs of Hell."[11] This is the deal that we make with God: if we acknowledge our brokenness and let go of even the smallest portion of our love of ourselves and earth, then we will find that we are healed. Lewis continues, "I believe, to be sure, that any man who reaches Heaven will find that what he abandoned (even in plucking out his right eye) has not been lost: that the kernel of what he was really seeking even in his most depraved wishes will be there, beyond expectation, waiting for him in 'the High Countries.'" The attempt to hold on to the notion that we are somehow "OK" or that we must prioritize our "esteem" is contrary to the offer of grace we find in the Scriptures. Jesus himself says, "Those who find their lives will lose them, and those who lose their lives because of me will find them" (Matthew 10:39). Understanding our total brokenness is one way that we lose our lives and then find them through God's grace on the other side.

The offer of grace that God offers us means our church services can't all be about nice and easy topics that ignore our brokenness. Brené Brown, the speaker and researcher on social work, went back to church hoping for it to be easy. What she found was that church wasn't supposed to be easy. She says that the "church was not an epidural for me at all, it was like a midwife who just stood next to me saying, 'Push, it's supposed to hurt a little bit.' "[12] Acknowledging our brokenness and total corruption hurts sometimes, but it is the core of our salvation. We make a disastrous move in the church when we confuse the fact that we are loved for the notion that we aren't in need of healing. We can't accept God's offer of grace if we don't think we need it.

Amazing Grace

The pairing of grace with our complete sinfulness is beautifully expressed in the most famous song on the matter, "Amazing Grace" by John Newton. The phrase "that saved a wretch like me" and ideas like "I once was lost" are not metaphors for Newton, but a complete awareness of his brokenness and sin. Newton, before finding the grace of God, was involved in the Atlantic slave trade. Thirty-four years after he quit working for the slave trade, he wrote in a public pamphlet arguing for the elimination of the slave trade, this is "a confession, which…comes too late….It will always be a subject of humiliating reflection to me, that I was once an active instrument in a business at which my heart now shudders."[13] It is fitting that the man who wrote so compellingly about God's grace could do so because he knew that he truly was a wretch.

Amazing grace! How sweet the sound
that saved a wretch like me!
I once was lost, but now am found;
was blind, but now I see.

'Twas grace that taught my heart to fear,
and grace my fears relieved;
how precious did that grace appear
the hour I first believed.

Through many dangers, toils and snares,
I have already come;
'tis grace hath brought me safe thus far,
and grace will lead me home.

The Lord has promised good to me,
his word my hope secures;
he will my shield and portion be,
as long as life endures.

Yea, when this flesh and heart shall fail,
and mortal life shall cease,
I shall possess, within the veil,
a life of joy and peace.

When we've been there ten thousand years,
bright shining as the sun,
we've no less days to sing God's praise
than when we'd first begun.[14]

6

How Can I Connect with God?

The Spiritual Question and Its Importance Today

Hurricane Harvey flooded Houston in 2017, and many Christians performed heroic deeds to help their neighbors cope with the disaster. One United Methodist pastor told Scott about his attempt to help someone who lived on a flooded street with the waters rising. The pastor and some church members used a boat to go down the street and approach the house. The pastor knocked on the door, introduced himself, and offered to rescue an older man. At first, the man did not want to leave, believing that the waters would soon stop rising. The rescuer explained that there was real danger and that evacuating sooner rather than later would be the best course of action. Then the resident asked who had sent the boat and learned it was a United Methodist team. The homeowner said, "I'm a Baptist. I think I'll wait for a Baptist boat to come by." The United Methodist rescuer responded, "You know, if I were a Methodist in a home that was about to be flooded and a Baptist boat came along, I think I'd go ahead and get in it." Finally, the homeowner agreed to get in the boat.

This true story mirrors a joke we have told over the years about a man who was relying on God to save him from a flood. He declined a car, a boat, and a helicopter trying to rescue him from the rising water, believing that

God would answer his prayers and save him. He died. When he got to heaven he angrily confronted God, asking why God had not rescued him. "What do you mean?" asked God. "I sent you a car, a boat, and a helicopter."

Like the people whose homes are threatened by flood, human beings are in spiritual danger. However, many people are in denial and do not believe that their spiritual problems are very serious, if they exist at all. The first step on the road of salvation is being convinced of our sin and acknowledging that we need God. The Alcoholics Anonymous group that Scott supported as a pastor had a saying: "You can't help a drunk." By that they meant you could only help someone who had "bottomed out" and was ready to admit that he was an alcoholic and powerless to fix his problem by himself. We saw in chapter 5 that all of us are sinners. We are all spiritually sick and in need of healing. The first step is to recognize that we have a problem.

God's help in the form of grace comes
to us in practical, tangible ways—
in much the same way as a boat is a practical
means of saving someone from a flood.

But the second step is finding help. Some people believe that they can solve their problems themselves. They often underestimate the depth of the problem or overestimate their own capacities. Christianity emphasizes that we are not left to ourselves—God exists and God is the best source of help. We also emphasize that God's help in the form of grace comes to us in practical, tangible ways—in much the same way as a boat is a practical means of saving someone from a flood. The question for people who are seeking help from God is, what form does God's help take? How can I connect with God? If God is real, how do I get access to God?

The Bible's Teaching

Wesleyans read the whole Bible as the account of a loving God who creates the world and then acts to save it. God created the universe and humanity, and called it good. He was saddened by human disobedience but did not give up on his creation. Instead, God chose Abraham and Sarah and gave them a special role in this plan to save all of humanity. He said,

"I will make of you a great nation and will bless you. I will make your name respected, and you will be a blessing.

I will bless those who bless you,
those who curse you I will curse;
all the families of the earth
will be blessed because of you."

(Genesis 12:2-3)

Abraham and Sarah had Isaac, who became the father of Jacob. Jacob's name was changed to Israel, and God's promises were carried through to the descendants of Israel. Over time and through the difficulties of slavery in Egypt, the people of Israel learned more about God and how to worship him and avail themselves of God's blessings.

God made himself available to
the Israelites physically through the laws
and the commandments that he gave them.

The Exodus from Egypt was a crucial turning point in the history of God's chosen people. God selected Moses as their leader, and Moses delivered to the Israelites the message he heard from God:

"I've clearly seen my people oppressed in Egypt. I've heard their cry of injustice because of their slave masters. I know about their pain. I've come down to rescue them from the Egyptians in order to take them out of that land and bring them to a good and broad land, a land that's full of milk and honey"

(Exodus 3:7-8).

God made himself available to the Israelites physically through the laws and the commandments that he gave them. The commandments given in

Exodus, Numbers, Leviticus, and Deuteronomy provided those avenues to connect with God. He gave them instructions for creating a dwelling for God's presence, a place of worship where they could connect with God as they wandered in the wilderness. He gave them instructions for building an ark of acacia wood that would be the focal point of their religion. He created the priesthood and set the tribe of Levi apart to lead the worship life of the people. All these commandments and instructions (which are easily skipped when reading the Bible) are in fact ways of connecting God's people to God.

The connection to God became more formal once the people of Israel settled in their land. The leaders set up sanctuaries in holy places, such as Bethel and Shiloh, so that people could seek out God when needed. Under King Solomon, a temple was built in Jerusalem and it became the center of worship. It was the home of the ark of the covenant and a place where sacrifices were made in accordance with God's commandments.

The temple was the focal point for access to God for hundreds of years. When it was destroyed in the Babylonian invasion in 587 BC, the Israelite people faced a crisis: if worship and obedience to God's commandments (and therefore connection to God) were centered on the temple in Jerusalem, how should they continue when the temple was no more? The Babylonians took the leadership of the nation into exile. Psalm 137 records the despair and the crisis the people of Judah experienced:

> Alongside Babylon's streams,
>   there we sat down,
>   crying because we remembered Zion.
> We hung our lyres up
>   in the trees there
>   because that's where our captors asked us to sing;
>   our tormentors requested songs of joy:
>   "Sing us a song about Zion!" they said.
> But how could we possibly sing
>   the LORD's song on foreign soil?
>
> (Psalm 137:1-4)

How could the people worship the Lord "on foreign soil" now that they were disconnected from their land and the temple was destroyed? It was during the Exile that the synagogue was developed as a gathering of the people for prayer to God. Eventually the people returned from exile and the temple was rebuilt. But gathering in the synagogues, observance of Sabbath, and other commandments remained important ways to connect with God. During Jesus' time the second temple existed, and we see him and the disciples following the standard practices of worship and sacrifice there. Worship in synagogues also continued, expanding access to God's word. For example, Jesus visited the synagogue in his hometown of Nazareth. Luke says, "Jesus went to Nazareth, where he had been raised. On the Sabbath he went to the synagogue as he normally did and stood up to read" (Luke 4:16). The same is true for Sabbath-keeping and observance of the food laws—these remained important ways to connect with God in Jesus' day.

The first disciples were all Jews who continued to obey all of the Old Testament laws and to worship in their synagogues or at the temple. The crisis came when Gentiles became Christians, and the apostles met in Jerusalem to determine if these new converts first had to become Jews in order to be Christians. As we discussed in chapter 4, it was determined that they had to follow the moral law but not the ceremonial laws of the Old Testament. This meant Gentile Christians did not worship in the synagogue on the Jewish Sabbath either. Christian communities began gathering on the Lord's Day, which is Sunday.

Two ceremonies eventually became central to Christian worship as ways to connect with God. First was baptism. John was baptizing people before Jesus' ministry began, and Jesus himself submitted to be baptized. By the time of Paul, baptism was a normal practice for entry into Christian discipleship. Jesus commanded his followers to "make disciples of all nations, baptizing them in the name of the Father and of the Son and of the Holy Spirit" (Matthew 28:19). The account of Peter's Pentecost sermon in Acts 2 includes the admonition, "Repent, and be baptized every one of you in the name of Jesus Christ so that your sins may be forgiven; and you will receive the gift of the Holy Spirit" (Acts 2:38 NRSV). When Paul is addressing the internal tensions of the church at Corinth, he makes reference to their history of baptisms:

> *My brothers and sisters, Chloe's people gave me some information about you, that you're fighting with each other. What I mean is this: that each one of you says, "I belong to Paul," "I belong to Apollos," "I belong to Cephas," "I belong to Christ." Has Christ been divided? Was Paul crucified for you, or were you baptized in Paul's name? Thank God that*

I didn't baptize any of you, except Crispus and Gaius, so that nobody can say that you were baptized in my name! Oh, I baptized the house of Stephanas too. Otherwise, I don't know if I baptized anyone else.

(1 Corinthians 1:11-16)

Paul makes it clear in Galatians 3:27 and elsewhere that baptism is "into Christ." While Christians have different practices and customs for baptism (for instance, infants versus adults and sprinkling versus immersion), the Scriptures intend for baptism to be the primary initiation into the Christian church and a key way that people are connected with Jesus.

The second ceremony of Christian worship in the earliest period of the church was Holy Communion. Sometimes called the Lord's Supper or the Eucharist, it was a practice of re-enacting the Last Supper. Luke describes the supper, saying, "After taking the bread and giving thanks, he broke it and gave it to them, saying, 'This is my body, which is given for you. Do this in remembrance of me' " (Luke 22:19). Within a few decades, the practice became standard for all (or at least most) Christians, and Paul could rehearse for the Corinthians both what he taught them and how they were not practicing it correctly. He admonished them for eating a private meal with some of them getting drunk. He then wrote,

I received a tradition from the Lord, which I also handed on to you: on the night on which he was betrayed, the Lord Jesus took bread. After giving thanks, he broke it and said, "This is my body, which is for you; do this to remember me." He did the same thing with the cup, after they had eaten, saying, "This cup is the new covenant in my blood. Every time you drink it, do this to remember me." Every time you eat this bread and drink this cup, you broadcast the death of the Lord until he comes.

(1 Corinthians 11:23-26)

These two ceremonies—baptism and Communion—
came to be called sacraments,
"outward and visible signs of an inward
and spiritual grace" that connect us to God.

These two ceremonies—baptism and Communion—came to be called sacraments, "outward and visible signs of an inward and spiritual grace" that connect us to God. For several centuries, there was a lot of debate about how many of the Christian practices were sacraments. While most Protestants hold to only these two practices, by the late Middle Ages the Roman Catholic Church determined that five additional practices should also be seen as sacraments: confirmation, penance (now called reconciliation), extreme unction (or anointing of the sick), ordination, and marriage. Protestants maintained that in Scripture Christ only commanded two sacraments, baptism and Communion, both of which connect us to Jesus.

Wesley's Answer

Before Methodism was established, Wesley was involved with a group called the Fetter Lane Society. A dispute arose about whether it was important or even necessary to receive Holy Communion. Within this dispute, a group called the "quietists" urged that people should not use the means of grace, especially Holy Communion, until they had genuine faith. This led Wesley to break with the group and form a new society at the Foundery. His sermon "The Means of Grace" was published several years later as a way of emphasizing how Methodists were to connect with God's saving power through Communion and other ways.

The text given for the sermon is Malachi 3:7, which reads in the King James Version, "Ye are gone away from mine ordinances, and have not kept them." Wesley does not use this verse in his sermon except to appropriate one of its words in his opening question, "But are there any 'ordinances' now, since life and immortality were brought to light by the gospel?"

He begins by claiming that the whole question would never have arisen in the early church, because it was universally accepted that Christ had ordained certain outward practices as a way of receiving God's grace. But over time some people began to pay more attention to the means than to the end. The goal of all Christian practices is a transformed heart—one that loves God fully and loves one's neighbor as oneself. The abuse of the means of grace had led to an overemphasis on the act rather than the heart. In reaction, some people began to focus on the other extreme and suggest that one can have faith and a transformed heart without these practices. As usual, Wesley is occupying the extreme center, holding both the practices and their goal of heart transformation in tension.

The goal of all Christian practices is a transformed heart—one that loves God fully and loves one's neighbor as oneself.

In asking whether there are any means of grace, Wesley gives a definition of what he means by the term: "outward signs, words, or actions ordained of God, and appointed for this end—to be the ordinary channels whereby he might convey to men preventing, justifying, or sanctifying grace."[1] Wesley does not mean to limit God's power to act—God's grace can come to people in many different ways. But he is asking about the channels God has established as "the ordinary channels," which can be trusted by believers on a regular basis. He lists three such means in this sermon: prayer, searching the Scriptures, and the Lord's Supper.

Christ commanded us to pray in Matthew 7:7-8 where he says, "Ask, and you will receive. Search, and you will find. Knock, and the door will be opened to you. For everyone who asks, receives. Whoever seeks, finds. And to everyone who knocks, the door is opened." Wesley refers to this and a number of other Scriptures, including the parable of the unjust judge in Luke 18. He also makes clear that he is referring to both public and private prayer as means of God's grace.

The second means of grace is "searching the Scriptures." Here Wesley quotes John 5:39 in the King James Version, "Search the scriptures; for in them ye think ye have eternal life: and they are they which testify of me." He also notes that Timothy was raised knowing the Old Testament from childhood and that Paul's letter to him says that "All Scripture is given by inspiration of God" (2 Timothy 3:16 KJV). Wesley believes that the written word of God—the Bible—is a primary way in which God communicates God's word to humanity. Wesley uses the phrase "search the scriptures" to emphasize the importance of reading the Bible and he quotes the Letter to

Timothy to show that it is trustworthy. Thus, people who are seeking God's grace should read the Bible.

Wesley deals with the objection that the John 5 passage is not truly a commandment but a statement of fact. He examines the Greek and calls the alternative reading "shamelessly false." The problem with this argument, as Wesley well knows, is that the Greek word can be translated as either the present indicative (statement of fact that they did search) or present imperative (they must search). It suits his purpose to claim it as a commandment for the purposes of this sermon—searching the Scriptures is a means of grace that Christ himself directed us to practice. But the ambiguity of the Greek explains why different English versions have both translations.

The third means of grace is to receive the Lord's Supper. Wesley quotes the account Paul gives in 1 Corinthians 11:23-26 and the interpretation in 1 Corinthians 10:16 that the cup is the communion of the blood of Christ and the bread is the communion of the body of Christ. Wesley then concludes:

> Is not the eating of that bread, and the drinking of that cup, the outward, visible means whereby God conveys into our souls all that spiritual grace, that righteousness, and peace and joy in the Holy Ghost, which were purchased by the body of Christ once broken and the blood of Christ once shed for us? Let all, therefore, who truly desire the grace of God, eat of that bread and drink of that cup.[2]

In a related sermon written many years later, Wesley argues that "it is the duty of every Christian to receive the Lord's Supper as often as he can."[3]

Explaining how the sacrament works was a major area of dispute during the Reformation. During that time, Roman Catholics solidified their teaching about transubstantiation, the belief that the Communion ritual changes the bread and wine into the actual body and blood of Christ. At the other end of the spectrum, some Protestants argued that the elements are mere symbols and are essentially unchanged. The Wesley brothers held to a middle-ground position sometimes called "real presence." Charles Wesley wrote a hymn explaining this approach, rejecting the Catholic view but teaching that the bread and wine are changed in the sacrament to convey God's power (referred to as "virtue").

O the depth of love divine, the unfathomable grace!
Who shall say how bread and wine God into us conveys!
How the bread his flesh imparts, how the wine transmits His blood,
fills his faithful people's hearts with all the life of God!

Let the wisest mortals show how we the grace receive;
feeble elements bestow a power not theirs to give.
Who explains the wondrous way, how through these the virtue came?
These the virtue did convey, yet still remain the same.

How can spirits heavenward rise, by earthly matter fed,
drink herewith divine supplies and eat immortal bread?
Ask the Father's wisdom how: Christ who did the means ordain;
angels round our altars bow to search it out, in vain.

Sure and real is the grace, the manner be unknown;
only meet us in thy ways and perfect us in one.
Let us taste the heavenly powers, Lord, we ask for nothing more.
Thine to bless, 'tis only ours to wonder and adore.[4]

As we see in this hymn, there is a sense of mystery about how the sacrament works but high confidence in its life-transforming effect. The Wesley brothers were modern people who believed that bread remains bread and is not magically transformed into something different. The medieval doctrine of transubstantiation made no sense to them. Communion bread still tastes and feels like bread; the wine remains wine. At the same time, they knew that people experienced God's grace in powerful ways through the sacrament. This transformative experience could only be explained by the grace of God that the bread and wine somehow convey. The Wesleys cannot explain the mechanism, but they testify to the reality of the grace conveyed to the believer in the sacrament.

The sermon "Means of Grace" lists three means, but two additional ones are mentioned in other places. In 1743, Wesley published the General Rules of the United Societies. These three rules were specifications of behaviors that would show the genuine desire of members of the Methodist Societies to be saved from their sins. These rules are still part of the doctrinal standards of The United Methodist Church.

First: By doing no harm...

Secondly: By doing good...

Thirdly: By attending upon all the ordinances of God; such are:

    The public worship of God.

    The ministry of the Word, either read or expounded.

    The Supper of the Lord.

    Family and private prayer.

    Searching the Scriptures.

    Fasting or abstinence.[5]

Note that fasting is included in the list. In the sermon "Upon Our Lord's Sermon on the Mount, VII" Wesley gives many reasons why fasting is a means of grace.[6] He argues that it focuses our mind on our relationship with God and is a help to prayer. He cites examples from the Old and New Testaments that our spiritual forefathers and foremothers practiced fasting. But the most important reason is that Christ commanded us by telling us how to fast. Wesley said, "For the commanding us to do anything *thus* is an unquestionable command to do that thing; seeing it is impossible to perform it *thus* if it be not performed *at all*."[7]

The Methodist movement also published decisions made by their annual conferences in *The Large Minutes*. Starting in 1763, Wesley lists Christian conference as a means of grace that is commanded by Christ. By this he means the kind of conversation that happens in small groups whereby people's faith is strengthened and they grow in grace.[8] Considered together then, Wesley's writings specifically identify five means of grace: prayer (public and private); searching the Scriptures; Holy Communion; fasting; and Christian conference or what today we might call small groups.

In all of this discussion, the role of baptism is unclear. In eighteenth-century England, Wesley could presume that all of his audience had been baptized as infants. The Church of England was established, and it was the normal practice to baptize a child within days of its birth. This was the occasion for giving the child her Christian name, hence the practice of calling it "christening." There were not birth certificates other than the baptismal register of the parish church.

Wesley taught that an infant is "born again" by water and the spirit at baptism. But he also believed that almost everyone has sinned away that new birth and stands in need of conversion again. In the sermon "The Marks of the New Birth," he urges baptized people to be born again and claim the benefits of conversion.[9] In a country where everyone has been baptized and when baptism cannot be repeated, it makes no sense to urge baptism as a means of grace to be claimed by his readers. However, in today's context where infant baptism is less universal, we can recognize baptism as a means of grace consistent with Wesley's understanding. Its status as a sacrament establishes its importance as a way of connecting with God's saving power.

The Wesleyan Way of Salvation

The Wesleyan way of salvation is a journey on which the believer first recognizes one's sin, repents, enters the Christian life, and then makes progress toward the goal of perfect love. On this journey, we know we are saved by grace through faith. God's grace is his love that makes possible each step we take on the journey.

The practical question, then, is what do we do? We know we need God's grace, so how do we get it? How do we connect with God?

> We connect with God by engaging in the practices that allow God to have the biggest impact on our lives—prayer, reading the Bible, receiving Communion, fasting, and gathering with other Christians. These means of grace open us to the transformation that the Holy Spirit will bring about in our hearts and lives.

Wesley's answer is to stay focused on the goal of allowing God to shape our hearts, minds, and behavior to become the kind of people God has called us to be. Over time we should love God more fully and love our neighbor and ourselves more fully. We connect with God by engaging in the practices that allow God to have the biggest impact on our lives—prayer, reading the Bible, receiving Communion, fasting, and gathering with other Christians. These means of grace open us to the transformation that the Holy Spirit will bring about in our hearts and lives.

In chapter 3 we mentioned Arthur's friend who committed his life to Christ and then wondered "What do I do now?" A wise friend would have said the following:

> You are on a journey to grow up into a mature disciple of Jesus. You need God's help in that process, but God is not going to force you along the way. Thus, you need to find ways of connecting with God's power to change yourself. Here is what you do:
>
> - Join a local church community where you will find other believers who are on the way. They will support you, guide you and make the journey with you. Every Christian always belongs to a local church.
> - Attend worship at least weekly. In the worship of God, we remind ourselves of who we are and who God is.
> - Receive Holy Communion as often as possible.
> - Read your Bible daily, both by yourself and with others. Listen carefully as the Scriptures are read in worship and expounded in the sermon.
> - Join in a small group for Bible study and Christian conferencing.
> - Practice the works of mercy that will show your concern for those who are in need.

We must always remember that practicing the faith in this way is not the goal of discipleship. These are means to connect with God's grace aiming at the goal of a transformed heart that loves God and neighbor fully. In such practices we can confidently expect to receive the grace of God.

Come, Sinners, to the Gospel Feast

The Lord's Supper is a feast through which God's love is shared. In it we draw close to the Lord and receive his grace. All of us are sinners who are hungry for spiritual food.

Come, sinners, to the gospel feast,
let every soul be Jesus' guest.
Ye need not one be left behind,
for God hath bid all humankind.

Do not begin to make excuse;
ah! do not you his grace refuse;
your worldly cares and pleasures leave,
and take what Jesus hath to give.

Come and partake the gospel feast,
be saved from sin, in Jesus rest;
O taste the goodness of our God,
and eat his flesh and drink his blood.

See him set forth before your eyes;
behold the bleeding sacrifice;
his offered love make haste to embrace,
and freely now be saved by grace.

Ye who believe his record true
shall sup with him and he with you;
come to the feast, be saved from sin,
for Jesus waits to take you in.[10]

7

Why Is the Christian Life So Hard?

The Spiritual Question and Its Importance Today

Why is there a gap between the example of Jesus and those who follow Jesus? If a real Christian faith results in a transformed life, why can we find so many counterexamples? We have met too many people who remain nasty and unpleasant months, or years, or decades after they became a Christian. If we look at our own lives, we see that once we make the decision to follow Jesus, it doesn't automatically make us kind and loving. Our baptism or conversion doesn't change our personality or our vices—it simply changes our relationship to God. Most of us know from experience that adapting who we are to who we should become is not easy. As the confession in the United Methodist Communion liturgy states:

> We have not done your will,
> we have broken your law,
> we have rebelled against your love,
> we have not loved our neighbors,
> and we have not heard the cry of the needy.[1]

If we are honest about our own hearts and lives, we know that we are broken. Our sins may be private and known only by us, but they are real. Being who Jesus calls us to be is very hard.

This gap, between the high standard of Jesus and our actual lives, is so apparent that it is expressed by both Christians and non-Christians. In *The Christ of the Indian Road*, E. Stanley Jones quoted a "kindly old philosopher of India, Bara Dada," who said, "Jesus is ideal and wonderful, but you Christians—you are not like him."[2] People we have known have admitted that they would be more likely to follow Jesus, except they don't always want to hang out with other people who follow Jesus. This assessment of Christians is very similar to a quote from Brennan Manning made famous by DC Talk as it opens their song "What If I Stumble": "The greatest single cause of atheism in the world today is Christians who acknowledge Jesus with their lips then walk out the door and deny him by their lifestyle. That is what an unbelieving world simply finds unbelievable."[3] This is the holiness gap. Jesus is holy; we are broken. It is a large and seemingly insurmountable gap.

Why is the Christian life so hard? And more importantly, given that it is so hard, are we ready to do the hard work of ridding ourselves of our sin and becoming more like Jesus?

The holiness gap is so overwhelming that many have given up trying to close it. We once saw a bumper sticker that announced this acceptance of our sinful selves to the rest of the world when it read, "I'm not perfect, I'm just forgiven." This seems to us to be an excuse not to attempt holiness. It would be like someone who doesn't have an immune system saying that they are fine because if they get an infection, they can always take antibiotics. We have a colleague and friend who recently died after a struggle with leukemia, where the cancer destroyed his ability to have an immune system. This friend was told often that he did not have any infection anywhere in his body, but not having an infection did not mean that he was well. True health is more than just a lack of an infection. If you know people who have gone through cancer, you recognize that the healing process is rarely easy. It takes work and effort to be healed. In the fifth chapter, we introduced one metaphor of

Jesus as physician—someone to heal the chronic illness of sin. And as with any chronic illness, healing is a process that takes time and struggle. But that leads us to wonder, Why exactly is that process so difficult? Why is the Christian life so hard? And more importantly, given that it is so hard, are we ready to do the hard work of ridding ourselves of our sin and becoming more like Jesus?

The Bible's Teaching

As we saw in chapter 1, the Bible's message is that the kingdom of God is real and has come to earth. This carries with it the expectation that this heavenly kingdom is to become real and make a difference in our lives. The biblical way of describing just how the kingdom becomes real and makes a difference in our lives is through the language of repentance. Throughout the Bible, repentance is how we turn toward God.

Jesus' first proclamation is that the kingdom of God is not simply something that exists, but a reality that demands something from us.

Repentance is a central part of Jesus' message from the outset. The earliest written story about Jesus' ministry comes from the Gospel of Mark, with minimal preface. While Matthew and Luke tell the genealogy and cultural context of Jesus' birth and the Gospel of John gives a more theological account of Jesus' life, Mark opens with only two reference points for Jesus' ministry. The first is a quotation from Isaiah 40, in which the prophet writes that God will send a messenger and that we must make ready for the Lord (Mark 1: 2-3; Isaiah 40:3). The second is the witness of John the Baptist, which echoes the promise that God is going to send someone who will have great power (Mark 1:4-8). In telling of John's ministry, Mark writes that his primary message is "proclaiming a baptism of repentance for the forgiveness of sins" (Mark 1:4 NRSV). Jesus, the one prophesied by both Isaiah and John, continues this message. "Jesus came to Galilee, proclaiming the good news of God, and saying, 'The time is fulfilled, and the kingdom of God has come near;

repent, and believe in the good news' " (Mark 1:14-15 NRSV). Repentance is at the heart of Jesus' message as well as John's. The first written account of Jesus' ministry shows the good news of God, promised since Isaiah, results in the need for us to repent. Jesus' first proclamation is that the kingdom of God is not simply something that exists, but a reality that demands something from us.

What exactly does it demand of us? What does repentance in the Bible entail? The Greek word used in this chapter of Mark is the word *metanoeo*, which means to change one's mind. This indicates more than simply a need to ask forgiveness; it includes an inner change. The Common English Bible translation, for instance, has translated that one word as "change your hearts and lives" (Mark 1:4 and 1:15) instead of the one word "repent." This translation captures both the inward (hearts) and outward (lives) aspects of repentance.

In the Old Testament, the Hebrew word usually translated "repent" is *shub*, which means to return. The easiest way to understand the Old Testament concept of repentance is in the Book of Jonah, where *shub* (returning) becomes the larger story of both Jonah and Nineveh. In the story, God asks Jonah to go to Nineveh and preach against it. Instead of doing what God asks, Jonah flees in the opposite direction. Through the intervention of a large fish that eats Jonah, he returned back to God both physically and spiritually through the prayer that he prays in the belly of the fish (Jonah 2). Jonah then goes to Nineveh, proclaims the judgment of God, and the city repents! They return (*shub*) to God, as the king strips himself of his clothes and, as a sign of his repentance, puts on mourning clothes and sits in ashes. Then the king calls the whole city to fast. God ends up changing his mind—God turns away (*shub*) from God's previous plan about the destruction of Nineveh (Jonah 3:9-10). The Book of Jonah is a lesson in what repentance really means—it is about turning a different direction. It is more than just seeking forgiveness in the moment; it is returning to God by going a different direction from where you've been headed. It's similar to the New Testament idea of repentance; when Jesus says to repent, he is asking for more than merely forgiveness, but a complete turning of our lives in a different direction.

As another example of repentance, consider the Old Testament Book of Ezekiel. It was written during the beginning of the Babylonian Exile, after generations of Israelites and Israelite leaders had been following the wrong path. You can read the accounts in the books of 1 and 2 Kings, and with a few notable exceptions like King Hezekiah and King Josiah, by the time of Ezekiel they had been going down the wrong path for a long time. Speaking to Ezekiel, God calls attention to the people's long-standing unwillingness to turn to God: "But the house of Israel will not listen to you, for they are not willing to listen to me; because all the house of Israel have a hard forehead and a stubborn heart" (Ezekiel 3:7 NRSV). Ezekiel's message was the same as what Jesus preached in Mark 1:

> Yet the house of Israel says, "My Lord's way doesn't measure up." Is it my ways that don't measure up? Isn't it your ways that don't measure up, house of Israel? Therefore, I will judge each of you according to your ways, house of Israel. This is what the LORD God says. Turn, turn away from all your sins. Don't let them be sinful obstacles for you. Abandon all of your repeated sins. Make yourselves a new heart and a new spirit. Why should you die, house of Israel? I most certainly don't want anyone to die! This is what the LORD God says. Change your ways, and live!
> (Ezekiel 18:29-32)

Ezekiel's testimony is that the gap between God and humanity isn't God's fault, but ours. Repentance is about turning away from sins—not just a forgiveness from them, but an abandoning of that way of life. The promise also is more than just forgiveness; it is "a new heart and a new spirit." Repentance includes the promise of a heart transplant, which is promised again in Ezekiel 36:26: "I will give you a new heart and put a new spirit in you. I will remove your stony heart from your body and replace it with a living one." Even after a long time of running away from God, the hope of God is a literal turning back toward God that will involve a changed heart.

Repentance is about turning away from sins—not just a forgiveness from them, but an abandoning of that way of life. The promise also is more than just forgiveness; it is "a new heart and a new spirit."

The exception of King Josiah in 2 Kings 22–23 and 2 Chronicles 34–35 gives us a look at what a full repentance looks like. The prior kings "did what was evil in the Lord's eyes" (2 Kings 21:2), culminating in the particularly detestable leadership of Josiah's grandfather Manasseh, who "led them into doing even more evil than the nations the Lord had wiped out before the Israelites" (2 Kings 21:9). In renovating the temple, the priests of Josiah's time discovered the book of the covenant, which scholars today usually identify with a portion of Deuteronomy. When the priests brought the document to Josiah, he read it and quickly realized that the people of Israel and Judah had not lived up to God's commandments and thereby had broken the covenant God made with them. Second Kings tells us that "as soon as the king heard what the Instruction scroll said, he ripped his clothes" (2 Kings 22:11).

Notice how similar this demonstration is to the king of Nineveh in the Book of Jonah. The word of God came to Josiah that "because you ripped your clothes and cried before me, I have listened to you, declares the Lord" (2 Kings 22:19). Josiah kept the commandments of God, returning the people to a celebration of the Passover festival, tearing down shrines and altars to other gods and illicit sites of worshiping Israel's God. God blessed Josiah because he not only asked for forgiveness, but turned the direction of his people back to God.

The Bible also depicts repentance on a personal level. In chapter 5, we told the story of King David's repentance after he had slept with Bathsheba and murdered her husband, Uriah. David's adultery and murder demonstrate that brokenness and sinfulness exist within even the best of humanity. His repentance came after the prophet Nathan came to him and pointed out his sin. Psalm 51 expresses David's repentance in powerful, poetic language. The psalm opens by identifying itself as "A psalm of David, when the prophet Nathan came to him just after he had been with Bathsheba." The words that follow reveal the depths of a truly repentant heart:

> *Purify me with hyssop and I will be clean;*
> *wash me and I will be whiter than snow.*
> *Let me hear joy and celebration again;*
> *let the bones you crushed rejoice once more.*
> *Hide your face from my sins;*
> *wipe away all my guilty deeds!*

Create a clean heart for me, God;
put a new, faithful spirit deep inside me!
(Psalm 51:7-10)

Jesus' understanding of repentance derives from this expectation to have a clean heart. His Sermon on the Mount in the Gospel of Matthew begins with a series of statements about happiness, including the proclamation that "Happy are people who have pure hearts, because they will see God" (Matthew 5:8). Jesus makes clear in his sermon that we must have clean hearts, as he goes into explicit detail about things like murder and adultery. The goal is not to merely avoid murder and adultery, but to have new hearts. Clearly, murder is unacceptable throughout Scripture, but Jesus also tells us, "I say to you that everyone who is angry with their brother or sister will be in danger of judgment" (Matthew 5:22). Likewise, it is not enough simply to avoid committing adultery; Jesus tells us that "every man who looks at a woman lustfully has already committed adultery in his heart" (Matthew 5:28). God doesn't want people who simply refrain from evil actions but who are transformed in their hearts.

God doesn't want people who simply refrain from evil actions but who are transformed in their hearts.

Jesus' challengers in the Gospels did not seem to understand that the goal of a life devoted to God is to have transformed hearts. Jesus tells the Pharisees that they are too focused on outside purity: "The Lord said to him, 'Now, you Pharisees clean the outside of the cup and platter, but your insides are stuffed with greed and wickedness. Foolish people! Didn't the one who made the outside also make the inside? Therefore, give to those in need from the core of who you are and you will be clean all over' " (Luke 11:39-41). Jesus was trying to teach about true repentance—a turning toward God that comes from the core of our hearts rather than affecting only our outward behaviors.

Jesus' followers, after his death, resurrection, and ascension, continued this expectation that repentance would turn our entire lives toward God. The goal of living a Christian life in the early church is about turning away from our broken selves and walking a path toward God. Paul asks the church in Philippi to "make my joy complete: be of the same mind, having the same love, being in full accord and of one mind" (Philippians 2:2 NRSV). In order to do that, Paul warns that the church in Philippi must turn from their former selves, saying, "Don't do anything for selfish purposes, but with humility think of others as better than yourselves" (Philippians 2:3). This goal is made even more daunting when Paul tells us that the bar that is set for their unified mind is Jesus; he tells them: "Let the same mind be in you that was in Christ Jesus" (Philippians 2:5 NRSV). According to both Paul and Jesus, the goal of the Christian life is to have the gap between humans and God closed—both in our actions and in our thoughts and hearts. The concept of repentance is so pervasive throughout Scripture because we humans often do not wish to close that gap.

One practical scriptural example of this difficulty comes from the Book of Galatians, where Paul contrasts actions that stem from selfish motives with the fruits of the Holy Spirit. This was a primary tool in our family as a guide for repentance. In Galatians 5:19-21, Paul writes that "The actions that are produced by selfish motives are obvious, since they include…doing whatever feels good…hate, fighting, obsession, losing your temper, competitive opposition, conflict, selfishness, group rivalry, jealousy…and other things like that. I warn you as I have already warned you, that those who do these kinds of things won't inherit God's kingdom." Raising children often results in the need to discipline them for actions such as those Paul describes.

True repentance is not simply about the past.

When Arthur or his siblings would fight and operate out of selfish motives and have conflict with each other, making things right would require more than an apology. The offending sibling would have to repent. He or she would be asked to quote Galatians 5:22-23, which comes right after Paul's list of self-centered behaviors: "But the fruit of the Spirit is love, joy, peace, patience, kindness, goodness, faithfulness, gentleness, and self-control." After the sibling named the fruit of the Spirit, another question would inevitably follow: "And which of these are you not living out right now?" The truth is that Arthur and his siblings did not wish to repent—apologizing and making it right is difficult. This Galatians passage taught Arthur and his siblings that true repentance is not simply about the past. It's about the future. It's about returning to who we are supposed to be no matter how difficult that process is. Paul closes this passage with the bold statement about the difficulty of the repentance path, that "those who belong to Christ Jesus have crucified the self with its passions and its desires" (Galatians 5:24). Crucifixion was not an easy path for Jesus, and it is not an easy path for us with our passions and desires. But it is the way that leads to a new and better life.

Repentance is something we must do again and again, even after we have gone through that gate for the first time.

Wesley's Answer

Wesley begins his sermon "The Repentance of Believers" with a quotation from Mark 1:15 where Jesus challenges the people of Israel to "repent...and believe the gospel" (KJV). Wesley notes that many people assume "repentance and faith are only the gate of religion; that they are necessary only at the beginning of our Christian course."[4] This metaphor of a gate is a helpful description of how we often talk about salvation. There are only two sides of a gate: the outside and the inside. Once you go through a gate, there is no need to go through it again. In the same way, we often understand salvation in terms of those saved and those not saved—we're either on one side of the gate or the other. Wesley's point is that if we view repentance only as a gate, it would only be needed once. What Wesley wants to make clear is that this understanding of repentance is too narrow. Repentance is something we must do again and again, even after we have gone through that gate for the first time.

Wesley opens his sermon by affirming that there is a repentance that happens at the beginning. His point is not that repentance isn't a gate at all; it's that repentance is a gate and more. We each need a first turn toward God. Wesley writes, "and this is undoubtedly true, that there is a repentance and a faith which are more especially necessary at the beginning: a repentance which is a conviction of our utter sinfulness and guiltiness and helplessness... and a faith whereby we receive the kingdom."[5] The first thing that Wesley wishes to do is to remind us that there is a gate—a way to receive the kingdom of God—and that this gate involves repentance.

This is a simple truth of Christianity— even when we give our lives to God, we are still broken. That brokenness doesn't mean our first repentance wasn't real; it means that our repentance isn't over.

Wesley's insight is that in addition to the idea of repentance and faith as a beginning part of our journey, it is also necessary as the journey continues. As he says, "there is also a repentance and faith... which are requisite after we have 'believed the gospel.' "[6] Repentance and faith are not merely the entrance, but also the way that we keep on the proper path toward God. Wesley defines repentance as "an inward change, a change of mind from sin to holiness."[7] When we first find faith in God, we often think of ourselves as now fully faithful Christians. We might assume that the sin we had before is now gone, since if we are truly repenting of our own sins, we "do not then feel any evil in our hearts."[8] As anyone who has gone through this type of transformation can attest, even though we truly believe in God and are Christians in that moment, our purity doesn't last. The sin in our hearts isn't fully gone. Wesley says that the sin "does not reign, but it does remain."[9] This is a simple truth of Christianity—even when we give our lives to God, we are still broken. That brokenness doesn't mean our first repentance wasn't real; it means that our repentance isn't over.

Almost as soon as we repent, then our own sin seeks to grab our hearts. Wesley assumes that the sin begins with pride, with being convinced that we are better than we are. This in turn leads to self-will and results in (and is its own form of) idolatry. We all begin to feel a "love of the world" that is contrary to the salvation that we have accepted. If we are honest, we soon recognize that Wesley is right: "We may therefore set it down as an undoubted truth that covetousness, together with pride, and self-will, and anger, remain in the hearts even of them that are justified."[10] Even when we are not actively sinning, we must also consider the sins that we do by doing nothing. Wesley tells the story of Archbishop Usher who "after all his labours for God" cried out in his final breath "Lord, forgive me my sins of omission."[11] Even a faithful bishop can still be guilty of remaining in (sometimes unintentional) sin.

But if we remain diseased even after we are justified and made right with God, we also know that God wishes us to be healed. As we saw above, this promise of healing is the grand story of the entire Scripture. Wesley points to the promise in Deuteronomy 30:6 that "then the LORD your God will circumcise your hearts and the hearts of your descendants so that you love the LORD your God with all your mind and with all your being in order that you may live"; and in the Psalms: "He is the one who will redeem Israel from all its sin" (Psalm 130:8); and in Ezekiel where God promises, "I will give you my spirit....I will save you from all your uncleanness" (Ezekiel 36:27, 29); and likewise in the Gospels where God says that we are able to serve God "in holiness and righteousness in God's eyes, / for as long as we live" (Luke 1:75). Thus, a complete healing is what God wants for us, but we have to believe it and seek it out. In the words of Wesley:

> This is the thing which you now long for: this is the faith which you now particularly need, namely, that the great physician, the lover of my soul, is willing to 'make me clean'. But is he willing to do this tomorrow or today? Let him answer for himself: 'Today if ye will hear my voice, harden not your hearts.' If you put it off till tomorrow, you 'harden your hearts'; you refuse to 'hear his voice'. Believe therefore that he is willing to save you today. He is willing to save you now. 'Behold now is the accepted time.' He now saith, 'Be thou clean!' Only believe and you will also immediately find, 'All things are possible to him that believeth.'[12]

Wesley emphasized a repentance for both nonbelievers and believers. For those who do not know of the saving grace of Jesus Christ, there is a need to repent and turn toward God for the first time. For those who are believers, repentance is still necessary for as we walk with Christ, sin is still in our hearts. We, too, must hear the call of Jesus to "repent and believe the gospel" as often as is necessary. The constant need for repentance is evidence of the difficulty of living like Jesus. For Wesley, our basic nature is not to love God and neighbor, and this is why the Christian life is so hard. But loving God and neighbor is what God wants for us; while the Christian life is hard, it is not impossible.

> The constant need for repentance is evidence of the difficulty of living like Jesus. For Wesley, our basic nature is not to love God and neighbor, and this is why the Christian life is so hard. But loving God and neighbor is what God wants for us; while the Christian life is hard, it is not impossible.

The Wesleyan Way of Salvation

As we have shown throughout this book, Wesley emphasizes both the need for a relative change (justification) in our relationship with God and a real change (sanctification). The faith traditions that have been sparked by John Wesley (including our own United Methodist Church) have sometimes downplayed the need for justification and that first repentance by which we turn toward God. Because we talk about faith as a journey and we believe that God can even be active in the lives of nonbelievers, we sometimes underemphasize the need for all people to have a saving faith in Jesus Christ. What we overlook when we do that is that our ability to be holy and sanctified is only possible after we are justified. The other approach is to assume that justification is all that is required and that our sins after we were baptized simply don't matter. This is not how Jesus interacted with his disciples—they were baptized and followed Jesus, and yet Jesus constantly taught them to continually improve in loving God and their neighbor. In the Lord's Prayer, he taught them to pray by seeking repentance: "Forgive us for the ways we have wronged you, / just as we also forgive those who have wronged us" (Matthew 6:12). The Wesleyan approach is to take Jesus and the commandments seriously. We must repent and believe the gospel, and that results in a life that fully loves God and neighbor. While God can and does work with all people, complete salvation requires repentance and a love of God. Jesus died and rose from the grave to change our status not only from unsaved to saved, but from broken to healed.

The Wesleyan approach is to take Jesus and the commandments seriously. We must repent and believe the gospel, and that results in a life that fully loves God and neighbor.

The antidote to our brokenness does not rest with us. The cure rests in us not only turning back toward God (relative change) but walking the righteous path to God and being made holy (real change). Scripture describes both steps in the one word, *repentance*. While Wesley, along with Scripture, is adamant that such healing is available to us today, in practice it requires a renewed commitment every day; our sins of pride and self-love are always lurking to come back into our lives. Wesley's own covenant prayer is one way we remind ourselves that our healing requires us to put all things in God's hands:

> I am no longer my own but thine.
> Put me to what thou wilt, rank me with whom thou wilt.
> Put me to doing, put me to suffering.
> Let me be employed by thee or laid aside for thee,

exalted for thee or brought low by thee.
Let me be full, let me be empty.
Let me have all things, let me have nothing.
I freely and heartily yield all things
to thy pleasure and disposal.
And now, O glorious and blessed God,
Father, Son and Holy Spirit,
thou art mine and I am thine. So be it.
And the covenant which I have made on earth,
let it be ratified in heaven.[13]

When we pray this prayer, it is a reminder of why it is so difficult for our lives to be fully like Jesus—it requires us to completely give up ourselves and what we wish. The difficulty of becoming holy and eliminating the gap between us and Jesus is not proof that it is impossible, but rather that it is necessary.

Depth of Mercy

"Depth of Mercy," written by Charles Wesley, tells the whole story of repentance. It begins with my own sin—"the chief of sinners"; acknowledges the grace of God and the constant failings of those that follow God—"I my Master have denied, I afresh have crucified"; and ends with the hope of complete healing—"Now my foul revolt deplore, weep, believe, and sin no more."

Depth of mercy! Can there be
mercy still reserved for me?
Can my God his wrath forbear,
me, the chief of sinners, spare?

I have long withstood his grace,
long provoked him to his face,
would not hearken to his calls,
grieved him by a thousand falls.

I my Master have denied,
I afresh have crucified,
oft profaned his hallowed name,
put him to an open shame.

There for me the Savior stands,
shows his wounds and spreads his hands.
God is love! I know, I feel;
Jesus weeps and loves me still.

Now incline me to repent,
let me now my sins lament,
now my foul revolt deplore,
weep, believe, and sin no more.[14]

8

What About My Money?

The Spiritual Question and Its Importance Today

By now, we hope you understand that the Wesleyan way is the Jesus way. This way takes seriously the whole of Scripture and the promise of a complete transformation and salvation through Jesus. That full transformation demands everything of us—our love, our energy, our passions, our life, and even our possessions. If we are as serious about our faith as Jesus asks of us, then nothing falls outside of the scope of our response to God's love. And as Wesley emphasized, that includes our money. Our money is an accurate and revealing test of our heart, as it is the place where we often get hung up. We are willing to give our time and some of our passion to God, but when we are called to invest our own money in the kingdom of God, it gets difficult. Even this chapter on money, in a context where we expect to be talking about "spiritual" things, can make us nervous and uncomfortable. That fact alone makes it all the more necessary to understand money as a spiritual matter.

Religious people talking about money conjures up images that give us convenient excuses to discount the importance of the topic. We think of mega-church pastors with private planes, and wonder whether religious talk about money is just the ruse of get-rich-quick charlatans. Or we see cult-like groups that demand money in exchange for spiritual conformity, and we think that religion must be a glorified pyramid scheme. The truth is that we are asked for money all the time from our churches and educational systems, and this is after we have paid our taxes. Everyone seems to be looking for a way to get more money. It makes us wonder whether the conversation about money in church is just one more group looking to get into what is ours.

For a moment, at least, forget the ways others approach money and reflect on your own life. How do you think about money? If you have what feels like enough (or more than enough) money, is it something that still occupies your attention every day? Does it make you feel secure? If you don't have what feels like enough money, is it something that you believe will provide security for you if you had it? If you are in debt, do you feel free? These questions and others like them help us realize just how deeply money influences our feelings of security and freedom and just how much our attitude toward money says about our spiritual priorities and well-being.

> A person's faith is intrinsically linked to how they view their money, because how they approach their money says something about what they trust and find important.

We prefer not to engage in conversations about our money because it is too important to us and its impermanence makes us nervous. This makes it the perfect lens to talk about the practical consequences of our faith. As pastors, we have seen that a person's faith is intrinsically linked to how they view their money, because how they approach their money says something about what they trust and find important. When you see money the way Jesus and Wesley did, you realize that this conversation is not about your church's budget or about anyone needing your wealth. The primary question about money is this: "Where do you put your trust?" The first seven chapters in this book describe the Bible's story of salvation and the kingdom of God, centered on questions at the heart of our spiritual life. This chapter is the test case—are we willing to put our resources where our heart should be? What about our money?

We know that a lot of pastors have talked about money, so we are lifting up the words of Forrest Pool, a member of Arthur's small group at St. Andrew, about his own journey. After tithing for five years and having it change his life for two years, Forrest decided to write down a manifesto entitled "Why I Tithe" which he shared with the church. He describes the pull of money like this:

> Money…During my life, it has been my least favorite thing, my strongest desire, my status symbol, my ticket to the social circle of my choice, my comfort, my stress, my love, and my salvation. It is power and weakness. But more than anything, for me, money has been about control. Money has been the one thing I could actually work harder and earn more of which would allow me to control "my situation." This is one reason talking about tithing has always struck a nerve with me. When anything is all of these things and more to a person, it is extremely personal. Money is personal. Tithing is personal.

Money is personal, and so is faith.

He continues by describing the way most of us approach money at church:

> The other reason I never liked hearing about tithing is because I didn't understand it. My understanding of tithing on the surface was: the church has to pay the air conditioning bill and needs money for the youth department. But my thought was always, "There are other rich people at the church that I am sure will step up to make sure the lights stay on if we don't have the money. So I'll just drop off five dollars and call it a week." If I thought the cause associated with the church offering was worthy, I gave to it in the same way I gave to United Way or a homeless guy at the stop light. I always heard about the "good" Christians who tithed regularly and thought it was kind of like they were paying their Christian membership dues. I saw it almost like paying the electric bill.

Forrest discovered that God didn't view money that same way. He writes:

> This is when God revealed to me that I was looking at tithing completely wrong, almost backwards. God did not intend for tithing to be a just another life expense. He did not want me to

feel uncomfortable when hearing about tithing at church. Rather, he desperately wanted to show me that there was so much more meaning behind the act than I ever knew. What changed in me is that I realized God asking me to tithe was not only an outward act used to fund the church, feed the poor, invest in missions, etc.; but for me, it was also an absolutely inward act aimed at releasing me from my number one idol. I realized that the reason I was so uncomfortable hearing preachers talk about tithing every Fall was because money was something I put before God.

The Bible's Teaching

The Bible begins with a conversation about resources. That's one way to understand the first Creation story in Genesis. "When God began to create the heavens and the earth—the earth was without shape or form" (Genesis 1:1-2). The story tells how God separated the night from day and the land from the sea, and how God created the animals and vegetation, culminating in the creation of humanity in God's own image. There would be no resources without God; it's all under God's domain. Our role, as creatures made in God's image, is to take charge of all of these resources:

> God blessed them and said to them, "Be fertile and multiply; fill the earth and master it. Take charge of the fish of the sea, the birds in the sky, and everything crawling on the ground." Then God said, "I now give to you all the plants on the earth that yield seeds and all the trees whose fruit produces its seeds within it. These will be your food. To all wildlife, to all the birds in the sky, and to everything crawling on the ground—to everything that breathes—I give all the green grasses for food." And that's what happened. God saw everything he had made: it was supremely good.
>
> (Genesis 1:28-31)

The biblical story tells us that every resource, plant, and animal in the entire universe is created by God and that this gift "was supremely good." Any response we make to God will come from God's first gift to us.

The first response to God takes place in the fourth chapter of Genesis with Adam and Eve's two sons: "Abel cared for the flocks, and Cain farmed the fertile land. Some time later, Cain presented an offering to the LORD from the land's crops while Abel presented his flock's oldest offspring with their fat" (Genesis 4:2-4). Likewise, Noah in the eighth chapter offers a gift back to God after he lands safely after the Flood:

Noah built an altar to the LORD. He took some of the clean large animals and some of the clean birds, and placed entirely burned offerings on the altar. The LORD smelled the pleasing scent, and the LORD thought to himself, I will not curse the fertile land anymore because of human beings since the ideas of the human mind are evil from their youth. I will never again destroy every living thing as I have done.

(Genesis 8:20-21)

These offerings are the first signs of a later practice of sacrifice to God, which we see among the patriarchs Abraham, Isaac, and Jacob and that came to be regulated by a set of commandments given to Moses. All of these practices recognize that it is right to offer back to God a portion of the resources that God gave us first.

All of these practices recognize that it is right to offer back to God a portion of the resources that God gave us first.

Later generations would clarify that our offerings are not to be the leftovers of what we have, but the first and best. In Exodus 23:19, the commandment is: "Bring the best of your land's early produce to the LORD your God's temple." A comprehensive instruction set is found in the Book of Nehemiah:

We will also bring the early produce of our soil and the early fruit from all trees every year to the LORD's house.

We will also bring the oldest offspring of our children and our cattle, as it is written in the Instruction, and the oldest males of our herds and flocks to our God's house, to the priests who serve in our God's house.

We will also bring the first of our dough, our contributions, the fruit of every tree, the wine, and the oil to the priests at the storerooms of our God's house. We will also bring one-tenth of the produce of our soil to the Levites, for it is the Levites who collect the tenth-part gifts in all the towns where we work.

(Nehemiah 10:35-37)

A portion of everything we have, from our produce, to our flocks, to our baked goods, is to go back to God. Proverbs 3:9 echoes Exodus and Nehemiah telling us to "honor the LORD with your wealth / and with the first of all your crops." Giving back resources to God, it implies, is wise.

The way we earn our resources and
the attitude we have toward them matter.

The Wisdom Literature in the Bible (especially Proverbs and Ecclesiastes) has instructions on our money that include more than our tithes and offerings to God. Proverbs begins, for instance, with an instruction from a father to a son, warning not to "let sinners entice you" if they are looking to ambush the innocent and "find all sorts of precious wealth" (Proverbs 1:10, 13). This instruction ends by warning that "These are the ways of all who seek unjust gain; / it costs them their lives" (Proverbs 1:19). Ecclesiastes warns us about our attitude toward money: "The money lover isn't satisfied with money; neither is the lover of wealth satisfied with income. This too is pointless" (Ecclesiastes 5:10). Evidently, the way we earn our resources and the attitude we have toward them matter.

The prophets also are not silent on the matter of our resources. Jeremiah, like Proverbs, warns us about ill-gotten gains: "Like a partridge gathering a brood that is not its own, / so are those who acquire their wealth corruptly. / By midlife it will be gone; / afterward they will look like fools" (Jeremiah 17:11). Ezekiel passes on words from God to the Prince of Tyre about his wealth, saying that "through your shrewd trading you multiplied your riches. But then you became proud of your riches" (Ezekiel 28:5). His pride in his money resulted in his death. Malachi, on the other hand, describes a positive vision for money: "Bring the full tithe into the storehouse, that there may be food in my house. And thereby put me to the test, says the LORD of hosts, if I will not open the windows of heaven for you and pour down for you a blessing until there is no more need" (Malachi 3:10 ESV). The Old Testament is filled with warnings and injunctions about our money, but also with descriptions of its proper use and the good that can result from it. Our offerings to God can result in a vision as grand as one where there is "no more need."

Jesus continues the conversation about money in the New Testament. Because the Gospels record conversations between Jesus and others, they feel more personal than the Old Testament's instructions and prophetic messages. Matthew 19:16-22 tells of a conversation between Jesus and a young man who "had many possessions." This young man asks Jesus "Teacher, what good thing must I do to have eternal life?" Jesus tells him to "keep the commandments," listing them out. The young man replies to Jesus that he has done this, and Jesus seems to throw down the highest challenge, saying, "If you want to be complete, go, sell what you own, and give the money to the poor. Then you will have treasure in heaven. And come follow me." It's important to recognize that this did not start out as a conversation about money. The man was asking about eternal life, and Jesus made it about money. By doing this, Jesus was communicating that our money and our eternal life are connected, which can be bad news if we are unprepared. The passage ends with an understandable and unfortunate reaction: "But when the young man heard this, he went away saddened, because he had many possessions."

The man was asking about eternal life, and Jesus made it about money. By doing this, Jesus was communicating that our money and our eternal life are connected.

Jesus cares deeply about what we do with our possessions, because it reveals what we prioritize. Out of thirty-eight parables Jesus told, sixteen of them were about money. In the Gospel of Luke, Jesus describes the connection between money and our heart:

> Whoever is faithful with little is also faithful with much, and the one who is dishonest with little is also dishonest with much. If you haven't been faithful with worldly wealth, who will trust you with true riches? If you haven't been faithful with someone else's property, who will give you your own? No household servant can serve two masters. Either you will hate the one and love the other, or you will be loyal to the one and have contempt for the other. You cannot serve God and wealth.
>
> *(Luke 16:10-13)*

Our money is a test of our faithfulness and our heart. Do we love God or our money? We can't love both.

The early leaders of the church took this challenge to love God more than our money seriously, as Acts tells us that "all the believers were united and shared everything. They would sell pieces of property and possessions and distribute the proceeds to everyone who needed them" (Acts 2:44-45). Timothy warns us that the "The love of money is the root of all kinds of evil" (1 Timothy 6:10). James perhaps has the strongest words, reminding the church that we will be judged by how we approach our wealth: "Pay attention, you wealthy people! Weep and moan over the miseries coming upon you. Your riches have rotted. Moths have destroyed your clothes. Your gold and silver have rusted, and their rust will be evidence against you" (James 5:1-3). From Genesis to the early church, the Bible consistently addresses how we approach our money because we often forget the foundational truth of Genesis 1: everything begins as God's, and one day we will be held to account for how we use what God has given us.

Wesley's Answer

Wesley's sermon "The Use of Money" begins with an obscure (and rarely preached) parable of Jesus from the Gospel of Luke about a manager who is about to be fired by his master (Luke 16:1-13). The manager decides to be dishonest and forgive his master's debtors, changing one man's debt of nine hundred gallons of olive oil to four hundred and fifty gallons, and changing another man's debt of one thousand bushels of wheat to eight hundred. This text is rarely used in sermons because Jesus seems to condone the work of the dishonest manager when he draws this conclusion: "I tell you, use worldly wealth to make friends for yourselves so that when it's gone, you will be welcomed into the eternal homes" (Luke 16:9). In Wesley's sermon, he notes that this passage takes place right after the "beautiful parable of the Prodigal son" which was a response to the grumbling that Jesus was spending time with sinners (Luke 15:2, 11-32). Jesus is telling the Pharisees and his disciples that they should not dismiss the "sinners" because "People who belong to this world are more clever in dealing with their peers than are people who belong to the light" (Luke 16:8). Wesley is using this parable as a lament that "spiritual" people are often not savvy enough about money and resources. If Jesus was highlighting the dishonest manager, then we who follow Jesus ought to be much more conscious of our resources and use them better.

> Wesley affirms that money can be used for noble goods: "In the hands of his children, it is food for the hungry, drink for the thirsty, raiment for the naked."

Wesley is adamant that money is not bad: "the fault does not lie in the money, but in them that use it."[1] It is not money, but the "love of money" that is the root of all kinds of evil. Poets, philosophers, and religious people have spoken out against money over and over again; but Wesley affirms that money can be used for noble goods: "In the hands of his children, it is food for the hungry, drink for the thirsty, raiment for the naked."[2] If we are to use the wisdom of Jesus and common sense, money can be put to its good and proper use. Wesley provides for us three essential rules for how we can be faithful with the gifts God has given us.

Wesley's first rule is, "gain all you can."[3] If money is not inherently bad, then surely earning it is not bad either. No one ought to feel guilty about the income they earn, as long as it is done in the right way. Wesley goes into explicit detail that we are not to make money at the expense of our life and health—that trade isn't worth it. We also should never make money in ways that hurt ourselves, our neighbors (including our employees), or our neighbors' (or employees') souls. If our gain comes in ways that avoid these evils, then there is no reason not to work hard and never procrastinate. Wesley says that this should be "by honest wisdom and unwearied diligence."[4]

Wesley's second rule is, "save all you can."[5] Do not waste it! Don't waste it on "idle expenses or desires of the flesh," by which he means gluttony or drunkenness. Don't waste it on pretending to be fancy, when true honor and value comes from God. Wesley instructs us not to waste money on our children if they are going to waste it. He calls giving excess money to children a "trap" for their souls because it allows them to waste it on "foolish and hurtful desires."[6] He further instructs us to only leave an inheritance for your children if you have trained them to be wise and generous with their money.[7]

Until this point, Wesley's teaching is no different than the words that you might hear from a secular financial adviser: gain and save as much money as you can. But these strategies, by themselves, are wholly insufficient and ignorant about the purpose for what we have been given. We receive gifts from God to do something with what we have been given. God has placed us here not as owners of the world, but as stewards of the world that God has made. A steward is someone who doesn't own property, but rather manages someone else's property. Thus, the third and most important of Wesley's rules is that once you have gained all you can and saved all you can, then "give all you can."[8]

Gain all you can.

Save all you can.

Give all you can.

What separates Wesley from standard church-preaching on giving is that he takes the normal instruction of a tithe and causes us to think differently about our money. Rather than simply saying that 10 percent is God's and the rest is ours, Wesley wants you to imagine all that you have as God's. First, take care of the things you need: food, clothes, house, and other necessities. Second, take care of your spouse, your family, and your community. Third, give to "the household of God." Fourth, give to others. Essentially, give all you can. Give more than the 10 percent, imagining all that you have as resources to be used for God's purposes. Wesley says, "Do not stint yourself...to this or that proportion. 'Render unto God,' not a tenth, not a third, not half, but 'all that is God's'" so that when you get to heaven you will be able to account for everything.[9] It is important for us to note that Wesley took his own advice. When he died, he had given almost all that he had away. The reason Wesley's words are so powerful is that he lived them, and he expected us to live them as well.

The Wesleyan Way of Salvation

Wesley's approach to money reminds us of a joke about creation. Scientists discovered how to create life, so they approached God. "We don't need you anymore—we know how you did it." God challenged them to demonstrate their wisdom, and so the scientists leaned down and began to form dirt into the shape of an animal. Immediately God stopped them, saying, "No, you need to get your own dirt."

When it comes to money and wealth, we often think we have created something—a business, or value for our company—when the reality is that all our resources that we are expanding and putting to use have come from God in the first place.

A proper approach to our money is the same as our approach to grace: it is all a gift from God. Money is simply the easiest and most powerful way to see whether we are structuring our life in a way that reflects our faith. The earliest accounts in the Old Testament tell of an offering to God. It was eventually clarified that such gifts ought to be a tenth of what we earn. If only we would all do this, it would be a great start. *Relevant* magazine gave us statistics that demonstrate how far the church is from truly living this way. Only 10 to 25 percent of a typical congregation tithes. More shocking, the authors noted that, "Christians are only giving at 2.5 percent per capita, while during the Great Depression they gave at a 3.3 percent rate."[10] But rather than beat people over the head with what they aren't doing, the article challenged us to imagine what could happen...

> if believers were to increase their giving to a minimum of, let's say, 10 percent. There would be an additional $165 billion for churches to use and distribute. The global impact would be phenomenal. Here's just a few things the Church could do with [that] kind of money:
>
> –$25 billion could relieve global hunger, starvation and deaths from preventable diseases in five years.
> –$12 billion could eliminate illiteracy in five years.
> –$15 billion could solve the world's water and sanitation issues, specifically at places in the world where 1 billion people live on less than $1 per day.
> –$1 billion could fully fund all overseas mission work.
> –$100–$110 billion would still be left over for additional ministry expansion.[11]

When Wesley says that in the right hands, money means food for the hungry and clothing for the naked, he meant this literally.

The place to begin is to start taking our money and resources as seriously as Jesus did. We must begin the practice of giving something to God. Many pastors begin by asking their congregation to give at an increasing percentage—1 percent this year, 2 percent next year, and so on. This may work for some, but it isn't what the Bible asks us to do. It asks us to begin at a tithe and imagine all that we have as belonging to God. We believe if people try to tithe, they will find themselves transformed. Rather than take our word for it, here is the conclusion of Forrest Pool's testimony quoted earlier:

> I realized that giving 10% of my income provides me a regular, tangible reminder that my purpose on this planet is not limited by the money I have. It became a commitment between God and me that my reliance on money would never again come between us. I realized that tithing was not a battle over my wallet (like I had always believed); it was a battle over my heart.
>
> What is crazy to me is, that since this realization, I continue to do the exact same act I did before of tithing 10%. But this new perspective has made it a completely different experience. This

realization and new view of tithing has blown open other parts of my spiritual life as well. It has helped me understand that things I have always done, and just assumed were the normal rules of being a Christian in this world, were actually God's intentional way of freeing me from this world.

I know we are all coming from different situations, backgrounds, and experiences, but this story is where I come from, and this is why I tithe.

He discovered what the Bible teaches: our hearts and our wallets are inextricably linked. If we wish to give our heart to God, we must be willing to give up our wallet.

O For a Thousand Tongues to Sing

We have chosen Charles Wesley's great hymn "O For a Thousand Tongues to Sing" for this chapter, even though it is not about money—it is about our hearts. If we can, with our whole heart, sing the praises of God that has set us free, then perhaps we can loosen the grip on our wallets.

O for a thousand tongues to sing
my great Redeemer's praise,
the glories of my God and King,
the triumphs of his grace!

My gracious Master and my God,
assist me to proclaim,
to spread through all the earth abroad
the honors of thy name.

Jesus! the name that charms our fears,
that bids our sorrows cease;
'tis music in the sinner's ears,
'tis life, and health, and peace.

He breaks the power of canceled sin,
he sets the prisoner free;
his blood can make the foulest clean;
his blood availed for me.

He speaks, and listening to his voice,
new life the dead receive;
the mournful, broken hearts rejoice,
the humble poor believe.

Hear him, ye deaf; his praise, ye dumb,
your loosened tongues employ;
ye blind, behold your Savior come,
and leap, ye lame, for joy.

In Christ, your head, you then shall know,
shall feel your sins forgiven;
anticipate your heaven below,
and own that love is heaven.[12]

Notes

Introduction

1. G. K. Chesterton, *Orthodoxy*. (Norwood, MA: The Plimpion Press, 1908), 144.

Chapter 1, "What Is the Bible's Message?"

1. *The Book of Discipline of The United Methodist Church*, 2016 (Nashville: The United Methodist Publishing House, 2016), ¶104, page 73. Hereafter referred to as *Book of Discipline*.
2. John Wesley, "The Way to the Kingdom," in *John Wesley's Sermons: An Anthology,* edited by Albert C. Outler and Richard P. Heitzenrater (Nashville: Abingdon Press, 1991), §I.12, 127. Hereafter referred to as *John Wesley's Sermons*.
3. "Love Divine, All Loves Excelling," words by Charles Wesley, 1747, in *The United Methodist Hymnal* (Nashville: The United Methodist Publishing House, 1989), 384. Hereafter referred to as *The UM Hymnal*.

Chapter 2, "How Can I Be Saved?"

1. "The Nicene Creed," in *The UM Hymnal*, 880.
2. John Wesley, "The Scripture Way of Salvation," in *John Wesley's Sermons*, §1, 372.
3. This echoes a quotation often attributed to Oliver Wendell Holmes: "For the simplicity that lies this side of complexity, I would not give a fig, but for the simplicity that lies on the other side of complexity, I would give my life."
4. John Wesley, "The Scripture Way of Salvation," §I.1, 372.
5. Wesley uses the term *preventing*. Today we normally use the word *prevenient*. Both refer to something that comes (Latin *veni*) before (*pre*).
6. "And Can It Be that I Should Gain," words by Charles Wesley, 1739, in *The UM Hymnal*, 363.

Chapter 3, "Am I a Real Christian?"

1. "Almost Christian: Q&A with Kenda Creasy Dean," interview by Terrace Crawford, Church Leaders, October 28, 2010. https://churchleaders.com/youth/youth-leaders-articles/145646-almost-christian-q-a-with-kenda-creasy-dean.html. Accessed May 6, 2018.

2. Kenda Creasy Dean, *Almost Christian: What the Faith of Our Teenagers Is Telling the American Church* (New York: Oxford University Press, 2010), 65.

3. Elie Wiesel, interview with Alvin P. Sanoff, "One Must Not Forget," *U.S. News & World Report,* October 27, 1986, 68.

4. J. Budziszewski, "The Second Tablet Project," in *First Things,* June 2002. https://www.firstthings.com/article/2002/06/the-second-tablet-project. Accessed May 6, 2018.

5. John Wesley, "The Almost Christian," in *John Wesley's Sermons,* §I.3, 65.

6. John Wesley, "The Almost Christian," in *John Wesley's Sermons,* §II.1, 65.

7. John Wesley, Journal Entry on "May 24, 1738," in *The Works of John Wesley*, Volume 18, *Journal and Diaries I* (1735-1738), edited by W. Reginald Ward and Richard P. Heitzenrater (Nashville: Abingdon, 1988), 250.

8. John Wesley, "The Almost Christian," in John Wesley's Sermons, §II.9, 67.

9. "Come, Let Us Use the Grace Divine," words by Charles Wesley, 1762, in *The UM Hymnal*, 606.

Chapter 4, "Do I Have to Obey the Law?"

1. *Book of Discipline,* ¶104, 67.

2. *Book of Discipline,* ¶104, 67.

3. John Wesley, "The Original, Nature, Properties and Use of the Law," in *John Wesley's Sermons,* §II.3, 259.

4. Ibid., §II.5, §II.6, 260.

5. John Wesley, "Upon Our Lord's Sermon on the Mount, V," in *John Wesley's Sermons,* §II.2-3, 210–211.

6. John Wesley, "The Law Established Through Faith, II," in John Wesley's Sermons, §I.2, 279.

7. Ibid., §II.1, 281.

8. Ibid., §§II.5-6, 282–83.

9. Ibid., §III.1, 283.

10. John Wesley, Notes Entry for Matthew 5:48, in *Explanatory Notes Upon the New Testament* (New York: Eaton & Mains, n.d.), 24.

11. "A Charge to Keep I Have," words by Charles Wesley, 1762, in *The UM Hymnal,* 413.

Chapter 5, "Am I a Sinner?"

1. Evan Marinofsky, "Participation Trophies Are the Worst Thing You Can Give a Kid," *The Odyssey Online,* September 7, 2016. https://www.theodysseyonline.com/participation-trophies-are-the-worst-thing-you-can-give-kid. Accessed May 7, 2018.

2. Betty Berdan, "Participation Trophies Send a Dangerous Message," *The New York Times,* October 6, 2016. https://www.nytimes.com/roomfordebate/2016/10/06/should-every-young-athlete-get-a-trophy/participation-trophies-send-a-dangerous-message. Accessed May 7, 2018.

3. Michael Long, "Fred Rogers, Quiet Radical: The Misunderstood Legacy of 'Mr. Rogers' Neighborhood,' " interview with Sarah Morice-Brubaker, *Salon,* July 31, 2015. https://www.salon.com/2015/07/31/fred_rogers_stealth_progressivism_the_enduring_legacy_of_mr_rogers_neighborhood_partner/. Accessed May 7, 2018.

4. Brené Brown, "The Power of Vulnerability," TED Talk at TEDxHouston, June 2010. https://www.ted.com/talks/brene_brown_on_vulnerability#t-1089050. Accessed May 7, 2018.

5. John Wesley, "Original Sin," in *John Wesley's Sermons*, §II.1, 328–29.

6. Ibid., §II.7, 330.

7. Ibid., §II.9, 331.

8. Ibid., §III.2, 333.

9. Ibid., §III.3, 333.

10. Ibid., §III.5, 334.

11. C. S. Lewis, *The Great Divorce* (HarperCollins, 2015), viii-ix.

12. Brené Brown, "Jesus Wept," *The Work of the People*. http://www.theworkofthepeople. com/jesus-wept. Accessed May 7, 2018.

13. John Newton, *Thoughts Upon the African Slave Trade*, quoted in Adam Hochschild, *Bury the Chains: The British Struggle to Abolish Slavery* (Pan Books, 2012), 130–31.

14. "Amazing Grace," words by John Newton, 1779, stanza 6 anonymous, in *The UM Hymnal*, 378.

Chapter 6, "How Can I Connect with God"?

1. John Wesley, "The Means of Grace," in *John Wesley's Sermons*, §II.1, 160.

2. John Wesley, "The Means of Grace," in *John Wesley's Sermons*, §III.12, 165.

3. John Wesley, "The Duty of Constant Communion," in *John Wesley's Sermons*, §1, 502.

4. "O the Depth of Love Divine," words by Charles Wesley, 1745, in *The UM Hymnal*, 627.

5. *Book of Discipline*, ¶104, 78–80.

6. John Wesley, "Upon Our Lord's Sermon on the Mount, VII," in *The Works of John Wesley*, 10:592–611.

7. Ibid., 10:604.

8. "The 'Large' Minutes, A and B (1753, 1763)," in *The Works of John Wesley*, 10:856.

9. John Wesley, "The Marks of New Birth," in *John Wesley's Sermons*, 182.

10. "Come, Sinners, to the Gospel Feast," words by Charles Wesley, 1747, in *The UM Hymnal*, 616.

Chapter 7, "Why Is the Christian Life So Hard?"

1. "A Service of Word and Table II," in *The UM Hymnal*, 12.

2. E. Stanley Jones, *The Christ of the Indian Road* (New York: Abingdon Press, 1925), 114.

3. Brennan Manning, quoted in DC Talk, *What If I Stumble* (Forefront Records, 1995).

4. John Wesley, "The Repentance of Believers," in *John Wesley's Sermons*, §1, 406.

5. Ibid., §2, 406.

6. Ibid., §3, 406.

7. Ibid., §I.1, 406.

8. Ibid., §I.2, 407.

9. Ibid., §I.2, 407.

10. Ibid., §I.9, 409.

11. Ibid., §I.14, 411.

12. Ibid., §II.3, 413-14.

13. "A Covenant Prayer in the Wesleyan Tradition," in *The UM Hymnal*, 607.
14. "Depth of Mercy," words by Charles Wesley, 1740, in *The UM Hymnal*, 355.

Chapter 8, "What About My Money?"

1. John Wesley, "The Use of Money," in *John Wesley's Sermons*, §2, 349.
2. Ibid., §2, 349.
3. Ibid., §I.1, 350.
4. Ibid., §II.1, 353.
5. Ibid., §II.1, 353.
6. Ibid., §II.7, 354.
7. Ibid., §II.8, 354.
8. Ibid., §III.1, 355.
9. Ibid., §III.6, 356.
10. Mike Holmes, "What Would Happen if the Church Tithed?" *Relevant*, March 8, 2016. https://relevantmagazine.com/love-and-money/what-would-happen-if-church-tithed. Accessed May 14, 2018.
11. Ibid.
12. "O For a Thousand Tongues to Sing," words by Charles Wesley, 1739, in *The UM Hymnal*, 57.

CPSIA information can be obtained
at www.ICGtesting.com
Printed in the USA
LVHW011915010922
727358LV00005B/30

9 781501 867934